Writing 36

CHARLES OLSON

the FIERY HUNT

and other plays

Four Seasons Foundation
Bolinas · California

"Apollonius of Tyana" was first published at Black Mountain College
in a limited edition in the summer of 1951, and was reprinted in *Origin*,
no. 6, 1952, and in *Human Universe and Other Essays*, 1965 and 1967.
It is reprinted here by permission of Grove Press, Inc.

Library of Congress Cataloging in Publication Data

Olson, Charles, 1910-1970.
    The fiery hunt & other plays.

    Includes bibliographical references.
    I. Title.
PS3529.L655F5 1977 812'.5'4 76-48311
ISBN 0-87704-034-6
ISBN 0-87704-033-8 pbk.

The publication of this book was supported by a grant from the National
Endowment for the Arts in Washington, D.C., a Federal agency created by
an Act of Congress in 1965.

The Writing Series is edited by Donald Allen, published by Four Seasons
Foundation and is distributed by Bookpeople, 2940 Seventh Street,
Berkeley, California 94710.

CONTENTS

INTRODUCTION

I.

This volume continues the effort to bring together the writings which Charles Olson left behind at his death in 1970. Presented here are the eleven known plays and verse dramas which he wrote during his career as poet. None was ever performed, a few were even abandoned before completion, but they all are notable for their willingness to explore the formal possibilities of theater.

Olson's interest in the theater extends back to at least his high school and college days, when he was a successful schoolboy actor, praised for his performances in such traditional entertainments as *Ten Nights in a Barroom*, *Gammer Gurton's Needle*, and Molière's *Doctor in Spite of Himself*, the leading role of which he played with "such ability and charm of acting that it is good to know that he is only beginning his academic career," one faculty member at Wesleyan University wrote in a review. He also took leading roles in community theater productions, formally studied theatrical skills at a well-run summer theater in a spacious old sail loft in Gloucester, and was himself assistant dramatic coach in addition to his teaching and debate-coaching duties at Clark University in his home town of Worcester in the early 1930s, leading discussions of Clifford Odets' protest classics *Awake and Sing* and *Waiting for Lefty* and directing performances of one-act plays by Eugene O'Neill. His earliest published attempt at dramatic writing appeared in the Wesleyan literary magazine and is the story of a Gloucester fishing family that loses its only son to the sea. Called *The Fish*

Weir, it is a melodramatic one-acter in the manner of O'Neill's
Ile.

So that, Olson was well acquainted with the traditional theatrical experience. As a youngster he saw the legendary Buffalo
Bill in his traveling Wild West show, and there was Clyde Beatty
the animal trainer in circuses at Stage Fort Park; later, he went
to the burlesque in Boston and in Hartford as often as he could
get away; and after he began his career as a poet he continued
to read conscientiously in the theater of the Greeks (Euripides
was his favorite) and in Shakespeare (in 1954 he wrote a number of chapters toward a book on Shakespeare). It was not un-
usual, then, that he should have tried writing for the theater
himself, as an occasional alternative to the opportunities a poem
might offer.

Olson's devotion to the dance goes back almost as far as his
interest in the theater and is wonderfully told by his college
roommate, John Finch (a few of whose own plays were later
performed with moderate success), in his reminiscence "Dancer
and Clerk" in the *Massachusetts Review* for winter 1971. Olson
enthusiastically attended the Ballet Russe whenever they gave
a performance in Boston, managing to get introduced to
Massine, its director, and even securing a walk-on part—as a
tree!—in a performance of Dali's *Bacchanale* in 1940.[1] But it
wasn't until meeting Erick Hawkins of the Martha Graham
company after a performance in Washington in 1948, and
especially not until Black Mountain, that Olson had the opportunity to work with dancers on an equal footing—notably
Merce Cunningham, whose classes he faithfully attended, and
Katherine Litz.[2] When the poet was asked to return to Black
Mountain for the summer of 1949 (he had delivered a series of
lectures there the previous fall as a replacement for Edward
Dahlberg), he was in the midst of rediscovering Homer's *Odyssey* through the French scholar Victor Bérard and exploring

with friends in Washington the possibility of a restored, but wholly original, Greek theater (including, plans were, an amphitheater built to scale in the Maryland countryside). He thus proposed in his letter of acceptance to Natasha Goldowski, acting head of the College at the time (4 June 1949), to teach a course in the *Odyssey*, which he stated "is the clue to the re-invention of new theatre . . . the mark of it the jointure of speech-sound-motion, projection-melody-gesture, one actor and chorus, central stage." Upon arriving he taught the course under the title "Verse & The Theatre," which was formally described as a "laboratory leading to a production at the end of eight weeks," in which were to be "re-examined and newly used" the relationships of "(1) dance composition to verse, without music; (2) to prose, ditto; (3) to solo instruments, chiefly woodwinds & percussion, the flute as well; (4) slides and color projections; (5) masks; (6) various combinations of the human voice, without music, without dance, but with gesture, posture, and the skill of speech." Olson himself produced that August an adaption from the *Odyssey* called *Kyklops* as well as a narrative from the Soninke folktales collected in Frobenius' *African Genesis*; other performances included *Atlantic Frantic* danced by Betty Jennerjahn, who is given a role in *The Born Dancer* in this volume, and Fielding Dawson's *Bazzball*.

But even before Black Mountain and while still at work on *Call Me Ishmael*, Olson considered the possibilities of both dance and drama as suitable to his needs. He wrote, 26 January 1945, in a notebook designated "KEY WEST I": "The Melville book also stands in this challenging position: narrative makes me impatient, but the possibility of taking what you last did and taking the images up out of the language and making them a series of dance masks . . . " (he proceeds to chart a series of conflicts which he has found in Melville). Earlier in the entry, in which he considers the possibility of retelling American folk-

tales the way Yeats retold Irish legends, he writes that such a
tale as that of Billy the Kid seems "endless & tiresome as narrative." "But," he adds, "it runs through me as *drama* – as dance
drama, perhaps, radio play (verse?), hardly straight theater. Why
is it that straight theater still seems necessarily contemporary-
realism? As do movies. Where dance & radio seems to permit
enlargements and poets' treatment?"

His writings continue to reveal the significance he found in
both drama and dance. As for the necessity of dance, Olson
points out in "A Syllabary for a Dancer," written at Black
Mountain for the Indian dancer Nataraj Vashi, that the Vedas
themselves define man in two ways: "*mana* as a thing which
thinks, and *nara* as 'root,' which, in its root means, you tell me,
to dance. Or, to transpose it, man is a thing which thinks and
dances . . . a dancing thinker, in other words, one who is capable of a technological mastery but who has forced his knowledge to a methodological result." (It might be said that these
plays for dancers seek to be such a result.) While in a letter to
editor Cid Corman, ca. 13 June 1952, Olson writes: "I believe
. . . that all men and women can dance – and this alone is
enough to establish expression – that all other expression is only
up from this base; and that to dance is to make a whole day
have glory . . . " Indeed, one of the instructions offered by Maximus is "how to dance / sitting down"; or, as Robert Duncan
noted in his poem, "The Dance," "Maximus calld us to dance
the Man." And it must be remembered that the ultimate reach
of "Projective Verse" is not for only a new poetics but "new
concepts from which some sort of drama . . . may emerge."
The examples Olson gives are not only the verse practiced by
"the sons of Pound and Williams," but plays such as *The Trojan
Women* and Seami's *Hagoromo*.

The dance-plays in this volume can be seen as attempts to
explore a sense of what drama might have been like before

the Greeks and the tradition of tragedy and comedy which descends from them. In the draft of a proposal seeking funds for the continuation of Black Mountain, Olson writes in early 1954, "the character of theater at Black Mt. is recognized to be *move-ment*, not literary theater"; and in his "Notes on Language and Theater" from that same time, he suggests that "drama and theater were *more* language & movement" (than character and plot) before the developments of the Greek stage. With Aeschy-lus, he argues, we have a second actor and dialogue, which lead to "the birth of that exaggerated individual called hero, and of that exaggerated narrative called tragedy," as well as to a divi-sion of language from movement. As with the language of Olson's poems, there seems always to be in his thought a twisting away from inherited, representational reality in an effort to recover an original energy and unity which has been lost to rational, civilized man, divided from nature and from himself.

The plays are what might best be called "experimental." Those that were written at Black Mountain reflect the super-abundance of creative energy at the college and the mingling of forms active there (the same forces that were to lead to what has sometimes been cited as one of the earliest "happenings," organized by John Cage in 1952). Olson saw the plays as exper-iments, opportunities to take advantage of the possibilities at Black Mountain. He wrote to Robert Creeley upon completing *Apollonius of Tyana*, "the place is overrun with talent for me to use, and learn by." They were composed with his character-istic inquisitiveness, and the search for an adequate, comfort-able, "projective" size for his own sizeable energies.

Olson never made any special claims for himself as a drama-tist. At Black Mountain or in speaking about the school, he always deferred to Robert Duncan, whose *Medea* was produced at the College in its very last days, as the playwright. It might

be said that Maximus was Olson's greatest dramatic voice and
that his letters, which the Maximus Poems began as, were his
proper stage. And it may well be that his own classroom or
lecture hall appearances, to those who were fortunate to have
experienced them, were finally his best performances and most
fully realized theatrical events. They certainly could be dramatic, like his self-possession in the face of a ranting, needling
Gregory Corso, who finally was summoned out of the room only
to get his nose punched and broken (by a librarian whom he
had insulted), leaving Olson to sort the chaos; or tossing hard
candies from the bag he had brought to class in an attempt
to cut back on his smoking; ordering a faculty wife out of class
and into banishment because "we are here for *work*, not for any
social occasion!"; untying the cashmere sweater from around
his waist and swathing his head in it like a turban, with prepos-
terous naturalness, to keep the ideas warm and coming; writing
on the blackboard and when room gave out continuing on the
wall, over the door and on to the other wall, until the point got
made; the bobbing walk, the Reindeer Dancer of Pleistocene,
or playing the front of the room for questions like the soccer
goalie he was in college. What it might have been like can still
be seen from his *Reading at Berkeley* (or better, the tapes of
that tour de force), or the reading he gives "The Librarian"
and "Letter 27 [withheld]" on the educational TV film, with
eyebrows wagging, widened eyes, all the gestures of the stage.[3]
It was dancing sitting down.

II.

Because all the plays in this volume except for *Apollonius of
Tyana* are published here for the first time, it is appropriate
to include some details concerning the individual texts. The
original manuscripts are preserved along with the rest of the
poet's papers in the Charles Olson Archives at the University
of Connecticut Library.

The Fiery Hunt, a choreographic script based on *Moby-Dick*, was written in April and May of 1948, a year after *Call Me Ishmael*, Olson's study of Melville, was published (the title was taken from the final lines of "The Whiteness of the Whale" chapter in *Moby-Dick*). It was not exactly or naturally a spinoff of the Melville book, but was commissioned by Erick Hawkins, whom Olson had met following his appearance in *Theatre Dance Pieces* performed as part of Robert Richman's Symposium on Contemporary Arts in Washington that March. (One of the pieces on the program was *John Brown: A Passion Play* based on the life of the revolutionary hero, with poetic script by Richman and two characters, as in *Fiery Hunt*, an Interlocutor and the main character of Brown danced by Hawkins.) Although it might seem that the project was undertaken to reveal the incandescent heart of *Moby-Dick* and the contraries of Melville's mind more directly or swiftly then the narrative and expository forms of *Call Me Ishmael* allowed, it was actually rather fully proposed to Olson by Hawkins. The title, the division into four parts, the characters (Ahab as protagonist and Ishmael as Chorus or interlocutor), indeed the psychologizing to be found within the piece, were all Hawkins' and present in the detailed outline he provided Olson with at the start. It was Hawkins' view that the Whale is not the true antagonist of Ahab but that the conflict is within his psyche, and he suggests in the outline that Ahab's character can be understood through Jungian terms — at a time when Olson had not yet read Jung with the persistence and belief he would ten years later. Hawkins provided the theme; Olson was to supply the language for the dancers, suffused with all that he had come to know of Melville as evidenced by his recent book. Hawkins was satisfied with what Olson wrote, but economic difficulties prevented *The Fiery Hunt* from being performed by the Graham Company, which was struggling to pay off creditors and make ends meet. Olson continued to have hopes for the play's production, inviting David Diamond, who had recently set some Melville poems to music, to compose a score for it; and later sent the play to Random House and to James Laughlin at New Directions to read it, but to no avail.

In the meantime, however, he continued on in the dramatic mode and wrote the first part of the mask called *Troilus* by July 1948. A difficult pregnancy which ended in his wife's hospitalization and a miscarriage proved too distracting and the play was never finished, although the following March he sent a copy to the young composer Frank Moore in the hope of resurrecting interest in it; but he wound up simply publishing a verse from it separately under the title "Troilus" (*Archaeologist of Morning,* p. [3]). Notes among the poet's papers indicate that this opening section – there called "The search for Love" – was to be the first of four parts (the remaining being titled, "the Attempt at love," "the Withdrawal from love," and concluding with "the Loss of love, the Triumph of love"), plus a short Epilogue in which the characters would appear "as they were at beginning but now the Chorus 1 & 2 are at well and the fountain better & T[roilus] & C[ressid] are in chorus position, both silent, back to the audience watching their young counterparts who do the speaking, leaving the question open: which way shall they go? Ahead? or repeat the older tragic characters?"

The Troilus of the mask is Chaucer's Troilus, and in notes for a talk entitled "The Search in Art, or Notes on the New Dimension" which Olson gave at American University on 29 July 1948, he reveals what interested him most about the figure. It was not only the romantic, star-crossed, double-crossed lover, but the Troilus who is the first Yuri Gagarin, the first astronaut – "the only man, so far as I know, who ever got a look at the whole world over his shoulder in one glance . . . he looked back from the seventh sphere and was able to see the earth in one glance." (Similarly discussed in "Notes for the Proposition: Man is Prospective," a lecture Olson was to give at Black Mountain shortly afterwards.) Troilus, then, is the embodiment of "prospective" man, Projective Man, and in that light the surviving first portion of the play ·falls considerably short of the point that Olson must have wanted to reach – the heightened moment when Troilus "takes the earth in under a single review" (the definition of "landscape" that Olson adopts in *Proprioception* and the Maximus Poems) in his quest for a unifying experience.

Following *Troilus* we have the outline for the proposed opera *Cabeza de Vaca*, which has survived as a two-page type-script, found separately among the poet's papers. It may have been drawn up as early as 1947, at the time Olson was working on his projected study of the American West to be called "Red, White, and Black," for which he was granted his second Guggenheim Fellowship and which was to be a series of narratives summarizing the settling of the West by the Red Indian, the European settler, and the Black slave. Toward that end, he attempted a rendering in his own words of Cabeza's *Narrative*, the account of the earliest white explorer to cross the Southwest, a heroic journey from Florida to northern Mexico, overcoming incredible hardships. Entitled "The Rime of Cabeza de Vaca," Olson's version was based on Cabeza's text as edited by Frederick W. Hodge in *Spanish Explorers in the Southern United States* (New York, 1907). The reader may also wish to see the poem, "The Story of an Olson & Bad Thing," written in June 1950 (in *Archaeologist of Morning*, pp. [14]-[20]).

Olson's next play, *The Born Dancer*, was written in the summer of 1951 after he had returned from the Yucatan to Black Mountain, with specific students at the College in mind, although there is no evidence it was ever performed. It is based on the life of Vaslav Nijinsky, the great Russian dancer, who had died in April of the previous year at the age of 60 and whose *Diary* Olson had read years earlier, judging from excerpts from it entered in a 1941 notebook. The episode of Nijinsky's encounter with the group of Russian soldiers (represented in the dance by The Russian Officer) had been reported by correspondent William Walton for *Life* magazine, 10 September 1945:

> . . . A few days later Nijinsky and a companion meandering through a wood came upon a barracks where Russian soldiers had gathered, singing around some balalaikas and an accordion. Nijinsky and his companion drew near and listened.
>
> "A little nip of vodka, tovarisch?" asked one of the soldiers, offering Nijinsky a bottle. He hesitated a moment, then said *"Da, da"* smilingly. The bottle went the rounds and came back again. Nijinsky took another swig of the potent stuff. The music waxed louder and wilder. Two soldiers were twirling and leaping in the sunshine. Suddenly between them rocketed the little grey-haired stranger in the tweed suit, leaping, twirling, executing incredible figures, so far outclassing the dancing soldiers that they stopped to watch. The musicians smiled and played harder.
>
> Soldiers shouted to comrades inside the barracks to come watch. They cheered and clapped. Few of these soldiers from the villages and steppes had ever been to Moscow, none had heard the name Nijinsky. But they recognized something tremendous in this pirouetting, leaping, dancing man who translated their familiar Russian music into whirling patterns of movement more beautiful than they had ever seen before.
>
> They cheered and clapped until he fell exhausted . . . .

(The story was also summarized in the *New York Times* obituary of the dancer, 9 April 1950, among other places.)

Of the other characters in the play, Romola was Nijinsky's wife, whom he had elected to marry rather than continue a rela-

tionship with Serge Diaghilev, the impresario. For thirty years
Romola devoted herself to trying to cure the schizophrenia
that had overtaken the dancer at the peak of his career in 1919.
Kyra, as the script indicates, was Nijinsky's daughter, herself
a dancer, and the "Spectre de la Rose" and "Petrouchka" were
two of his most famous roles. The text survives as a single four-
page carbon copy of a typescript, the original of which might
have been given to Tim LaFarge or one of the other dancers
for consideration.

This was followed by *Apollonius of Tyana*, written in late
July 1951 at Black Mountain and attractively published that
August at the College in a limited edition of fifty copies. It
was later reprinted, with slight revisions, from the Black
Mountain edition by Cid Corman in *Origin* 6 (summer 1952),
the text used here. No original manuscript appears to have survived. The play was drawn directly from G.R.S. Mead's life of
Apollonius (London, 1901), which Olson would somehow have
had at Black Mountain, although the figure of Apollonius had
been on his mind for a number of years as one of those nearly
forgotten embodiments of value like Cabeza de Vaca, as is mentioned in a letter to Robert Creeley, 27 July 1951, the day after
he finished the first version. It was written for Nicola Cernovich, who was to dance the leading role of Apollonius, while
Olson himself was to be Tyana, the speaking part. Cernovich,
a student at Black Mountain, had performed a dance to Olson's
poem "Pacific Lament" the previous winter while Olson was in
Washington and had written a Noh-inspired play which was
performed at the College in May of 1951 and published in *The
Black Mountain College Review* that June. A note in the first
edition indicates that Olson considered the text only "a DRAFT
of the materials, a blocking-out of the movements & words,"
but despite such a limitation, and Olson's sense that there still
remained (as he wrote to Corman on 12 August 1951) "a few

days' verse, to finish it," it is easily the poet's most accomplished dramatic piece and one of the more important vehicles of his thought.

Apollonius successfully conveys and summarizes a number of the poet's fundamental beliefs that are consistently held throughout his work — most notably, the primacy of the particular and the local, and along with that the supremacy of the "instant" as the proper arena for man — the basis of Olson's activism. It is also seemingly autobiographical, or at least with convenient parallels to the life of the man Olson ("He craved to talk . . . to get at things by talking about them. In fact, he was one of those who talked to live"; or, "He is now 40 years old, and at last aware of the dimension of his job . . . "), and of the author of the Maximus Poems ("He is almost foolishly 'local,' heavy with particulars, to the point of seeming a busybody" — as his Gloucester neighbor, Mrs. Tarantino, well knew (see *Maximus* III, 10)! — "a gossip, a flatterer, he is after things so." The play as read is a dramatic monologue like the Maximus Poems, or like Olson the writer of letters (almost daily to Robert Creeley at this time), the teacher, the orator addressing himself to the Ephesians, to his "fellow cits," "o Gloucesterman . . . kill kill kill kill kill / those / who advertise you / out." Apollonius is another attempt, like Cabeza and like Maximus or his prototype Bigmans, to create a persona to embody virtue, a model of value, a hero to stand forth as an "image of man," as Maximus says of himself, "even if the life appeared biographical." Apollonius is of Tyana the same way Maximus is of Tyre and Olson is of Gloucester — bound together, they are "an image of health in the world." The parallels are many and instructive, and include such keys to an understanding of Maximus as the passage where Apollonius "strikes at unity (and the immortalism he takes it such doctrine leads to) by teaching men everywhere, that what is native to themselves, even the places, heroes, and gods local to their neighborhoods, is worth all the state or world-religions they are being offered on every hand. And the clue to both attacks is his prime conviction, that no man should impose his mode of life on others."

Next, *Document* was dated 23 January 195[3] in manuscript, but never finished. In a letter to Robert Creeley written that same day, Olson speaks of coming "a cropper" on the play. "It went handsome for three pages, and then, when the figures (doublets, a speaker & a dancer) were engaged, I got bored." The Black Mountain dining hall for which the piece was written, a cavernous room with wooden posts, exposed beams, and a large fieldstone fireplace at one end, was the principal place for both scheduled and spontaneous dramatic performances at the College.

Telepinus was written in response to a suggestion made in July 1961 by Kindred McDade, the wife of a former FBI agent, who had returned to school and enthusiastically declared herself to be an admirer of Olson's writings, and who had some connection with the drama department at Manhattanville College, a somewhat exclusive Catholic women's college located in the northern suburbs of New York City. Olson did not turn to the play right away, but a typescript of *Telepinus* was sent her on 26 November 1961, and the play was immediately thrown into rehearsal, with Leon Katz, then a professor of dramatic arts at the school, as director. However, it was soon realized that it would likely prove offensive—with its references to the Virgin as "cherry / rosy & red"—not so much to the students and the nuns, but to the parents who had been invited to attend the benefit program at the college.[4] Olson was notified only at the last minute by telegram of the cancellation (a notice that the entertainment was performed appeared in *Poetry* magazine in February 1962, forgotten to be retracted). The play itself is based on the Hittite myth concerning the god of fertility,

Telepinus, like Christ—or Attis or Adonis or Osiris—a dying and reviving god.[5] His angry withdrawal from the earth leaves the world desolate, with both gods and men facing starvation, until he is finally appeased by gifts and praise and persuaded to go back home, so that life returns once more to the earth.

Fluff, a lightly spun drama of "competitive natures," exists as a typescript with a few penciled reworkings. It was written at the same time as the previous play, although an exact date is not available. It does not seem to have been sent Leon Katz as indicated.

White Isle, the last surviving play in the series written for Manhattanville, is drawn principally from book III of Pausanias in Frazer's splendid five-volume edition (sent Olson by Robert Creeley years before), with additional matter drawn from Frazer's extensive notes. The character of Neoptolemus, how-ever, would seem to derive from Sophocles' *Philoctetes*, al-though with some confusion: it was actually Philoctetes who had the noisome wound and was given charge of Hercules' bow, while Neoptolemus himself was the son of Achilles not of Hercules. Mimus, who is neither historical nor legendary, is simply the poet's adaption of Mimos (Greek 'mime'), who according to Olson in his "Notes on Language and Theater," "wasn't even imitation with the Grks— It was travesty . . . " The play survives in a typescript which had been sent McDade and returned, as well as an original holograph manuscript, which gives indication of having been written straight out, as a run, and then somewhat revised. A fourth play for Manhattanville, a rough sketch for a pantomime (called a "phantomime" in a letter to Donald Allen, 28 December 1961), based on the story of Gilgamesh, has not survived. Entitled "Dumb Show," evidence indicates it was sent McDade ca. 4 December 1961, who passed it on to Leon Katz.

The *Wild Man* fragment, which survives hastily written in

pencil only, is in the same tone as *Fluff* and was probably written around the same time. Perhaps these are all examples of the *saturos* or satyr-play—as Olson cites it in his "Notes on Language and Theater"—"a form we know nothing about."

And finally, there is *The Nineteenth of April*, which was begun some time between 1960 and 1963 but abandoned after five scenes. Like much of Olson's writing, it is Antaean, seeking to draw its strength from an earth of facts. It was a promising exercise, to take the familiar story of Paul Revere and attempt to "make history 'work,' " but he apparently lost interest in it or was unable to breathe life into the clay of materials, yet it had best be preserved with the rest of his dramatic attempts.

George F. Butterick

NOTES

1. Finch, who was there, remembers Olson's role as that of a giant; Olson told the editor in conversation in 1968 he was dressed as a tree, with tights and foliage.

2. Some sense of the Black Mountain climate at the time is offered by Mark Hedden in his "Notes on Theater at Black Mountain College (1948-1952)" in *Form* 9 (April 1969), as well as by Martin Duberman's *Black Mountain College: An Exploration in Community* (New York, 1972), esp. p. 370 ff.

3. Produced by Richard Moore for the National Educational Television series "USA: Poetry" in 1966, available from the Indiana University Audio-Visual Center.

4. Telephone interview with Leon Katz, 5 November 1974.

5. See James B. Pritchard, ed., *Ancient Near Eastern Texts Relating to the Old Testament*, 2d ed. (Princeton, 1955), pp. 126-128, and Theodor H. Gaster, *Thespis* (New York, 1950), pp. 295-315, who points out the ritual basis of the myth and its role in seasonal festivals. Both texts were known to Olson.

THE FIERY HUNT
and Other Plays

THE FIERY HUNT

A Dance in Four Parts for Two Men

for Erick Hawkins

Characters: AHAB and ISHMAEL

Stage: Two elements — (1) a *quarterdeck*, stage rear, with a broad taffrail behind, and some vertical (shrouds or mast) by which Ahab supports himself;

(2) a *whaleboat*, stage left, un-planked, its ribs suggesting bones as well as boat, with thwarts on which tubs may rest and Ahab sit high

Music: Four woodwinds, piano, percussion

The four parts to the action are:

I The Hunt

II The Descent

III The Return

IV The Death

There are four corresponding "hours." Where lighting is not possible to indicate these changes, a program note may be used, thus:

"The action takes place at four different hours,

AN END OF A DAY, A NIGHT, A NOON, A DAWN AND DAY."

Part I

THE HUNT

(It is an end of a day, if possible, light falling off.

Ahab is in his recurring place, his monomanic watchout position
at the rear, where there is a pivot hole in the deck for his whale-
bone leg. This time, however, he is turned the other way from
the usual, so that his right, trousered leg covers the bone leg
from the audience. He is looking out so that the audience sees
only a quarter of his face.

Ishmael, right stage, is squatted near the wings, as though lean-
ing against a hatch. He speaks, close to the audience, after a
pause once the curtain is drawn.)

ISHMAEL:
    I am Ishmael and he, there, on the quarterdeck, this whale-
    ship now moving in these midmost waters of the world, is
    Ahab, Captain Ahab, turned, as though he were, as he is, in
    truth, hidden, from you, from me, from the crew, hidden.

    It is the purpose, the purpose. But the intention
    (hidden, from himself too, hidden)
    what is the intention,
    where does the action go?

    We know the purpose, told us a Christmas gone:
    to hunt the seas until, no matter when
    we track a creature down,
    huge thing that once, in these same lonely waters
    swept the sickle of its lower jaw and reaped away
    like mower in a field of wheat
    this Ahab's leg; a whale, a white-hump whale
    who made that day one spot in blue Pacific red
    and Ahab from that day to stand on one live bone
    the other, whale, – and dead.

He rules, his will rules, flog us, steer us, command.
Yet our demand, three years, yet our demand:
under the water, under the barb, under the man,
where do you lead us,
where does the action go?

(AHAB stirs but continues to stand absorbed, his gaze fixed outward.)

ISHMAEL resumes, after thought, as though he were turning over the nature of this Ahab:
It was no accident. Ahab sought that whale
as men the fate they spin their egos toward.
His hate lived long before he lost his leg
and, lost, he merely found excuse
and object big enough to vent his hate upon.
And now, to prove that hate, he must, once more, seek out
  that whale
although he will on horn of self by self himself impale.

AHAB, at this point, turns slowly and, turning, reveals the leg for the first time. He starts to pace back and forth, tendering the leg as though he were now first using it after his accident, accenting his heel to make the illusion of a stump. At the same time the pacing is a marking, in footprints, of his one, unsleeping, everprowling thought.

ISHMAEL, as this walking begins to develop itself toward the instruments of the hunt, speaks these final lines of the introduction:
Vengeance we know, to one another, rivals, states
follies, stupidities, hates. But nature —
to attack nature, her creature, to turn the chalice
to find (in the sea, a fish, the sun) gesture, malice

(to break matter down and turn force to fire)
is it to lead, and if it is to lead, where   M
where does such vengeance go?   O
                                                                  V
                                                                  E
Under the water a hill of snow   M
o strange ungodly godlike man   E
where do you lead us, to what woe?   N
                                                                  T

By this time AHAB has worked himself forward and is at the
whaleboat examining the instruments of the chase, lifting the
harpoon slightly from its crotch (poised as it has been from the
beginning, pointed out at the audience), testing the sharpness of
its barb, picking up his quadrant to check it, perfecting the top
coil of the line in its tub.

It is the chart, however, that here provokes him, his idle examination of it leading him into THE DANCE OF THE CHART, his
anatomy of the pursuit. It is the *introductory* dance, serving
some of the same purpose as Ishmael's words up to now, but
focussed on the whale as the words were on Ahab.

ISHMAEL, before AHAB begins the dance, while he is at the
boat, speaks these short identifying lines, in a different voice,
anxiety, bitterness, and the first sign of his personal agony:

ISHMAEL
    We are no more to him than tools
    harpoon, quadrant, line, chart.
    His only care, he keep us sharp.
    Means, means. The end, the hunt only rules!

AHAB: THE DANCE OF THE CHART, which is both where the
whale is and with what mania Ahab pursues him and, at the
same time, through what maze and currents of himself he goes.
It is his dream of what this hunt will be and he is full of an assurance that he is as much as he thinks he is. For Ahab has some

image of himself as grand, some god-child wronged. He dances
the course he'll follow as though he will be triumphant, the god
he wishes he were, that this once in his life he will feel that he
has enough control of life to regard himself as originator,
source, father, before whom no one, instead of the disease of
forever remaining a son. It is the annunciative dance. "It is the
purpose."

ISHMAEL watches the dance with concentration, moving his
body in empathy to its changes but, in contrast to the imagined
kinetic of a spectator, he should convey the impression that he
has seen such a dance before and is in an advanced stage of
thought about it. His gestures (they should be no more) turn
out, questioningly. "The intention, what is the intention."

THE DANCE OF THE CHART dissolves into THE DANCE OF THE
HEAD and ISHMAEL marks it thus:
> As on the chart the tracings of the hunt
> so, on his forehead read, the lines and courses of the hate.

AHAB: THE DANCE OF THE HEAD. It is as though his dance
of the chart leads Ahab to the pondering of the nature of himself. It is an anatomy of evil.

It begins after Ahab has replaced the chart in the whaleboat and
has moved back toward his world of the quarterdeck, his inner
world where he broods and feeds. The idea behind it, behind
the head as the image of it, is the maddening attempt to get at
the why of the mystery, of himself and of his choice of the
whale as enemy. The movement is intellectual, cold, it is a
dance of the mind, the muscular equivalent the pushing against
a wall. It is a resistant, questioning, controlled dance, not the
mad degree of mind Ahab will yet reach. Ahab, here, in what is
essentially an abstract dance, is face to face with himself, still
sane.

Ahab's first movements (they coincide with Ishmael's couplet above) are of his hands to his head, his hands trying to hold, yet rub away, the burden of his growing mania. Then he starts his self consideration. Ishmael interprets his thought in the first lines below.

(These lines of Ishmael's run along the DANCE OF THE HEAD, play upon the same questions and dynamics as the dance itself, but, like the music, are counterpoint, not explication. Their sound and rhythm work, as well as their meaning, to do what the language has done in the introduction and must continue to do throughout — keep, by verse, the words raised up to the intensity of the music and the dance.

But they should be voiced in the least fashioned of Ishmael's three voices; much less "sung" than the higher intonation of the introduction [his high role, questioner, shaper of the critique], and less pitched than his third [himself, the individual crew member caught in Ahab's web]. Here is most the teller of the tale.)

ISHMAEL interprets Ahab's thought: D
    All his means are sane,   A
    it is his motive and his object that is mad.   N
                                                           C
                                                            E

                    AHAB, not in answer but on his own
                    track of thought, speaks his first
                    words of the play:
                        Mad? And if I am mad,
                        how, mad.   D
                                                  A
ISHMAEL: N
    Mad to wreak   C
    vengeance on   E
    a dumb beast!

AHAB:
>   Beast? No beast
>   but all the evil of this world!

ISHMAEL:
How, evil?

> D
> A
> N
> C
> E

AHAB:
>   I'd strike the sun
>   if it insulted me!

ISHMAEL (more to the audience):
There are such men who turn
the objects of this world into
the subjects of a kingdom called
themselves.

> D
> A
> N
> C
> E

AHAB:
>   I, I am the equal of them
>   evil, all!

(To which ISHMAEL opposes only
silence)

AHAB (after this pause, continuing his
dance of thought):
>   My mind's intact
>   My mind, my mind
>   intact, an emperor!

ISHMAEL (to audience):
True, my captain,
true, great brain!

> (AHAB
>   here
> dances out
> the memory of
> that agony
> and this
> triumph)

When he was struck he overcame
the danger to his mind.
His madness, equal strong, besieged
and took that mind and now together joined
they aim the concentrated cannon of himself

upon this one mad mark. So Ahab has,
to this one end, ten thousand time
the power were he
but mad or sane alone.

At which point both Ishmael and Ahab have arrived at a parallel
sense of Ahab's strength, Ishmael granting Ahab's powers despite his judgment of them, Ahab in intellectual command of
them (as he will not be in the next scene). So, as Ishmael de-
scribes the battle Ahab would join, Ahab dances it (the love of
evil, let me remark, being as much a part of it as any enmity).

ISHMAEL:

Forehead to forehead he'd confront the whale and,
locked in battle with it, put
an end to demonism, all
that lies around us like a snare, poised
to trick, laugh, mock, defeat
confound and ravin us, all
that torments, stirs, the truth with malice in it
of life, thought, impulse, objects, fear;
what he called once, what lies behind the pasteboard mask
and cried, "Strike . . .

AHAB:
Strike!

ISHMAEL:

. . . through the mask!"
and said, "How can the prisoner get out
except he thrust . . .

AHAB:
thrust!

ISHMAEL:

. . . through the wall!"

D
A
N
C
E

D
A
N
C
E

D
A
N
C
E

AHAB:
> the wall! the wall!
> The White Whale is that wall
> thrust up against me
> and my kind!

From which climax Ahab goes on to dance *after* Ishmael has
finished. It will depend, of course, upon how the choreography
feels, but I would suggest that Ahab arrive, with his last movement, well forward, at the bow of the whaleboat, foursquare
and proud, his mind's dance over, his eyes full of the vanity of
mind. There he looks out over the audience at all unseen things
such lesser people cannot see. It will give the audience their first
chance to see him face to face and size him up at rest.

From this pose I would have him break and make the transition
to Part II his movement back to the quarterdeck. Once there he
should take off his hat and coat and lie down on the taffrail as
though to sleep. And the lights, if there are any, go down gradually to night.

After Ahab is settled Ishmael also prepares for night, moving
slowly across stage, and throwing himself down at the bow of
the whaleboat. It is from this position that he speaks to open
Part II.

[Handwritten margin note, left side, rotated:] Judgement: Ahab's or Olson's?

[Handwritten note at bottom:] 31 MAR 91 Having difficulty with the "AT Sea" imagery. Roller coaster reading: Olson shifts from difficult to redundent; however powerful in showing evil possesing the man (by man's request) as opposed to man possesing evil.

Part II

THE DESCENT

(It is night. Ahab is stretched out on the taffrail, his left bone leg out stiff, Ishmael in semi-darkness against the whaleboat.

The music has enlarged itself in the caesura between I and II and has quieted again as the two men seem to have gone down into the night.)

But Ahab's *sleep of anguish* is soon on him, and the action is resumed, with a low moan from him, and his arm shooting up, and falling back limp across his body. He turns to find himself a better rest as Ishmael speaks.

ISHMAEL:
  His sleep is never rest, but further plotting of his course.
  The night's suspended as his day, as though the watch he kept
  abaft there on the deck, hoisted at times by basket to his mast,
  goes on in dark, his eye forever fixed on his intent.

  His soul and mind's split off from sense and heart,
  those planks men stand on when they're whole. Hung up,
  day-night a rope, he dreams not, knows not hope
  but wears, in poor exchange, anxiety for coat,
  nightmare to ride, and swings, in sun and out,
  Penduto of the cards, this Ahab, sign
  of man's more recent fall.

Ahab, during this speech, has once sat up in that startle of a person in a nightmare and stared fixedly at Ishmael as person will when they are not awake but seem so, and fix on someone near to break the spell. He continues to stare for a held moment, the torture that has started him clear in his eyes, and then falls back to stretch out as he was. Ahab, then, after the speech cries out:

He spouts! is red!

Stern all! I have his heart at last!

ISHMAEL:

Often so we hear him cry above us in the night

as though his own heat grew too much within him

At which point, his mad cry having energized the mare he rides, Ahab rises from the bed and rushes headlong into the NIGHT-MARE DANCE, described below, Ishmael continuing:

and, hot of himself, as though he were in fact fire's son,

he hurls himself against the dark and bursts his hot heart on it

like a shell, a star!

The dance itself is such explosion and the whole stage is suddenly shot with wildness, even Ishmael crying out his lines with an awe of superstition in them. For they should dart in and out of Ahab's action like flashes lighting up the dark of his behavior, somnambulistic and fierce as it is.

ISHMAEL:

They say he was not born as other men,

tell of the time he lay three days like dead

on passage of the Horn!

AHAB:

The Crown! the Crown!

D
A
N
C
E

ISHMAEL:

And in Nantucket there's a Gay Head squaw

who swears the livid white scar on his head

goes down his body to his toes!

AHAB:
> Fire! Father! Fire!

ISHMAEL:
> And he has done himself more grievous harm:
> not long before we set out on this mad voyage
> in some night rage he wheeled and drove
> his splintered stump into his other groin,
> was found upon the street like broken dog!

D
A
N
C
E

AHAB:
> till the sea itself shall
> lick my blood!

(The dance exploding more and more.)

ISHMAEL:
> Yet he goes on, wild, wild, protected as he falsely thinks
> by one prophetic claim by devil I'll not name
> who cried, to slake this Captain's appetite
> and slave him to his own consummate hate,
> "Hemp only, Ahab, only hemp will kill thee!"
> and Ahab finds security in this thought, blind of his scorn
>   and pride:
> "Ha! no gallows . . .

D
A
N
C
E

AHAB:
> No gallows!

ISHMAEL:
> . . . there are no gallows on this sea I ride!"

Ahab has come to climax and, as though the mention of the
hemp and his own voicing of the gallows had broken in through
the surface of his nightmare, gone down where it lodges in the
abyss of him, he abruptly, wrackingly comes awake. But the
seizure carries over as he puts on, almost like some numb thing,
his hat and coat again, the ritual of departure for the chase, and

then collapses, the leg here giving out under him as in like manner the hemp will jerk him out and down from the stance of life.

He falls, as he fell on the Nantucket street and as he will lie, for that split second, in the penultimate moment of this play, after he has been pulled out of his boat and before the line snaps him forever off the stage.

When Ahab breaks ISHMAEL lets out, without knowing it, as though he spoke for crew and all, a single cry, in prayer and warning:

Captain!

Captain!

and makes a move, as though to help the stricken man, but stops, as though he dare not and, instead, falls into song, as though to rest his Ahab, lead him back to sleep.

ISHMAEL:
 Learn, o Ahab, learn
 a man is man, no god
 thrown down

 Ahab, learn
 the wheel of man does turn
 (what gods there are
 man makes)
 and, turning, takes
 what once had light
 down,
 the great star's fall,
 to demon
 down.

O, Ahab, ego-hot, let go
let us again never know
your demon of display!
We are your children but defy
your own self-lie.
Brilliance earns you place with us
not separate in some sky

The song now does what Ishmael half-consciously intended,
brings Ahab's attention back to curative reality. With the next
stanza:

Put back to rest
your crew you've waked
turn your attention
down

Ahab rises and, as Ishmael finishes his song to bring the tension
of the scene down, Ahab does a parallel thing. A quiet, tender
dance issues out of him, as though he were brushing his charges
back to sleep. It is the godlike man to offset the mad, ungodly
one possession has made him in this part up to now.

ISHMAEL:
And while you do,   D
my hot old man,   A
hearken to   N
your orphan: C
                                                     E

the heat in us
is the life in us
and love the ends we put heat to,
generation or
creation

Learn, stubborn man
from another son
man's oldest, stubborn lesson:

    the life in us
    is the god in us
    and love a present heaven
    and hell of hate
    serves neither end,
    generation or
    creation.

D
A
N
C
E

Ishmael sleeps and Ahab returns to his monomanic place to watch out the night. The music completes the sense of dark.

Part III

THE RETURN

The hour is just short of noon and the light the full amber of a midday on ocean when the wind is soft and the waters calm. Ahab and his ship, Ishmael and the crew inhabit the physical world most directly at this moment, dwell in the heady ambience of sun, air, sperm, light, wood.

Ahab, in his familiar place, is not fixed in pose or gaze but stands relaxed, looks his whole world over at his ease, sun, ship, sea. He has returned from his dark and is starting in again on the pursuit, with another tempo, from another layer of his self. This is the daytime of his diabolism, and it is his body that now comes into play. Human madness is a cunning, feline thing. When you think it has fled, it has merely transfigured itself into a subtler mode.

After an abundant glance, to harvest all, Ahab moves forward with lightness and vigor to fetch his quadrant from its place in the whaleboat. Ishmael is seated cross-legged before a tub kneading lumps of spermaceti back into fluid state. It is one of the few delightful tasks the life of a whaleship allows.

AHAB's first eye is on Ishmael like a knife. Then, abruptly, with his quadrant swinging in his hand, he throws his glance up at the sun and, with a squint at it, addresses it thus:

> Sun, you hot old animal, I'd talk with thee!
> My sea-mark! My sea-mark, you can't turn away,
> for there you are, my slave, nailed to the sky,
> nailed like that coin of gold I've fastened to my mast
> reward for him who first shall sight the Whale!
> Nailed, sun, for my regard, mine, Ahab, who looks at you!

I'll look you in the eye, my wild red thing,
I, Ahab, will take your measure, I'll read you,
Sun, as full of mystery as you think you are,
coptic creature! Are you, are you so much more obscure
than the markings that Spaniard fashioned on my doubloon?
I'll have your meaning, I'll have your answer to my question,
you too will serve me, pilot, in this chase!

With these demands Ahab starts his QUADRANT DANCE. He
grasps the quadrant with both hands in front of him at the waist
and dances throughout as though it were the sun itself he held,
and it were obedient to him. It is a stately dance, more auto-
cratic than stately, and Ahab handles the quadrant assertively
(it is always at waist level, with his body pulled up from it). For
Ahab now seeks to declare himself lord of day's reality (he has a
league with the power of night) and wants to show he can shape
it any way he pleases. An instrument, a man, the sun, they are
all clay.

As Ahab starts to dance, ISHMAEL, though he is working with his
back to Ahab, moans out, with a high pitch in his voice:

Quadrant and doubloon, quadrant and doubloon
this man at noon can pitch us down!

But AHAB pays no heed, for he takes himself to be mighty, is
now demonstrating that he is, proving to himself and to the sun
that he, of all men, has power. He expresses it as phrases in the
dance:

Mountains are egos!
Towers are egos!
And you, Sun, are an ego!
All grand and lofty things!

For Ahab has transposed himself back to the moment when he
did nail the doubloon to the mast and he is interpreting the sun

as he then interpreted the coin, as if the sun had a face like the moon, features on it that can be read as he has read the coin — three peaks, and Ahab ruler over them, proud as a demon and full of scorn for lesser, human things.

ISHMAEL knows Ahab's purpose through the back of his head and sends out his warning:

> The sun's a coin but he reads it backward
> the sun's our gold but he sees it dark!

AHAB does not hear or care. He gives voice to his own will:

> Three peaks, I see three peaks
> and all, all as proud as I,
> as proud as
> Lucifer!

and he dances that will. He dances the three peaks down, the three peaks of the sun, reducing to his service the vital spirits of them, the three forms — a flame, a tower and the crowing cock. For there is a side to this dance which is the white reverse of black magic. Ahab is dancing a very ancient dance, a dance of sympathetic magic, in order to heap up, acquire for himself all the natural powers residing in natural things. It is the primordial dance of the Zodiac, and by it Ahab imagines he seizes the life and skills which the animals and images of the sun's year possess. He says it:

> The tower — is Ahab!
>   The volcano — is Ahab!
>   The crowing cock — is Ahab!
> All are Ahab!

And his body acts it out. His arms and legs are beak and talon by which he snatches the powers he wants, in this cockpit of his deck where he overcomes the sun. But his torso stays erect, for he is ruler, emperor of the sun, invested with its powers which he has now danced the acquisition of.

The end of the dance is Ahab's light leap into the bow of the whaleboat, where he seats himself high, swings the quadrant to his eye and, with his bone leg out over the gunwale, quietly awaits the sun to reach precise meridian.

ISHMAEL is one of the crew, is the crew, has been busy all this time over his tub, and now that Ahab has quieted down, he sings, and the other seamen in the row with him on the deck sing with him too, if you can hear them:

> Angels! angels! and this most fragrant spermaceti, mother me!
> Deprived, o sweet air!
> To play   to dip my hands in joy   to kiss
> o captain! what round cherry did you miss
> as boy, what tree that now you crave
> to make this mast our grave?
> To tie us to it, as to you, a stake
> and burn us as the olders do
> the youngsters in a game?   /

> Angels, angels and jars of sperm make sweet
> this womanless sea, this Ahab dry and bare!
> Come, heart, down, boy
> remind this man
> who must have that that's gentle hidden in him
> we live to love   to eat   to sleep   to work
> to see   and dream
> and ask him, in our name,
> who bullied him, what shame, that he forsake
> intention, and our claim?

Ahab keeps trying the sun with his quadrant during this song

> O angels with your hands in jars of sperm!
> o sun, bright coin of this most tender noon!
> Sing! sing to this Ahab, dance!

Woo him as some girl must have once
remind him, he was not born of woman
to destroy
he was not loved of woman
to betray
win him as the wind the sea today!

But this is not the hour that AHAB can be caught. His heart is
not quite shriveled up, but he has other business on his mind.
Ishmael's song does not reach through to him, and he punctuates
his own absorption in his purpose by speaking out again:

So, high and mighty pilot: you tell me where I *am*, most
    handily,
 but can you give me the smallest, least of hint of where I
    shall be?
Or, more to my purpose, where one other thing besides me is,
this living moment? Where, o mighty sun, where is — the
    Whale?

This instant you are eyeing him and he, perhaps, with that
    small eye,
that small, most evil eye of his, looks back at you.
My eye in turn looks into your eye, yet where he is your eye,
your round, full eye that looks on everything, can tell me
nothing, nothing, nothing, Sun!

And with that Ahab comes to his feet on a thwart and makes an
angry disposal of the sun by spinning his body as a discus
thrower does. His body erect, an axis, his bone leg raised to
whip him around, he hurls the disc of the sun away. In his own
mind, it is clear that he thinks he is superior to the sun, a
whirling fire in his own right, and that his body, where that fire
is, is more to be trusted to point out his course than any clue
he'll get from the sun. Or from his quadrant. He has come to
the decision. He'll trust himself to turn him to the true. He'll

have no more of the day's instruments, outer things. It is his
own sharp physical self he'll go by, make fine and temper it and
fit it as he can a needle for his binnacle. Dead reckoning.

> And you too my foolish toy, you, quadrant, can do no more,
>   not one jot more than can the sun. And yet, with your
>   impotence,
> you insult the sun by holding yourself up to it. Science, bah!

Ahab whirls again.

> I curse all things which turn men's eyes to heaven.
> God meant man to look out straight on his own level,
> as his eyes are, set in the front of his face.
> He did not put man's eyes on the top of his head
> like a bulb

and holds the quadrant on top of his own head, and pivots, to
make his point by mock. The gesture passed, he goes on:

> Curse thee, quadrant! No more by you I'll guide my earthly
>   way!

Ishmael, alarmed, turns from his tub and faces Ahab as he steps
to the gunwale and, with one foot on it, cries out:

> I'll look to my own horizon, not to gods' or the sun's
> or yours, quadrant!
> Away with you. And science. And false religion's goals!
> Away with you!

and Ahab hurls the quadrant down from him on to the deck. He
leaps after it, and dances it to pieces under his feet, crying:

> I'll trample you, you paltry thing, that feebly points on high!

Ishmael comes to his feet and Ahab, standing now bold and
defiant on his own deck, speaks on:

I'll use men's level things: my ship, my compass and these
   men.
I'll go by log and line. These shall conduct me and,
in this confusing sea, show me my place and destiny!

then, his voice enlarging, and with the gestures of a captain,

Man the mastheads! Call all hands up! Up helm!
It's a white whale, I say, a white whale!
Sharp! sharp! Skin your eyes! Look sharp for white water!
Square away!

and Ishmael leaps aft to keep excited lookout for the Whale
while Ahab lifts up the harpoon in his hand.

Part IV

THE DEATH

It is 6 A.M. All is wet from the night but it is the light which is strange. It makes Ahab, on the quarterdeck, to stand out huge. His back is turned and his whole body is large and black against the white horizon; in fact, in this light he makes a shape exactly like a black cross, for his arms are out from his shoulders as he holds the harpoon in front of him, lifted up like an offering, the barb of it showing high over his head.

When Ishmael comes on deck direct from sleep, he stops astonished at the sight. Ahab has such a dimension, is so much old man of oceans this morning that Ishmael at first takes him to be other than himself, to be some Vulcan come on deck out of the sea. He stares at him until he comprehends that Ahab has been there the night long and now stands, like some dark priest, waiting for only one thing, the day to bring his crew on deck so that he may consecrate the black mass he has contrived for them out of his night.

What ISHMAEL does not so easily understand is the peculiar atmosphere of the deck. For everything, himself, Ahab, the ship's elements, show sharp and unnatural. Suddenly the world around is the color of the whaleboat and the quarterdeck, the color of bleached bones. And there is a presence – falling in. He gives voice to it while Ahab holds where he is:

What whiteness is this that the night has left,
what added fear to what this man has brought?

Such light is holy in another place,
of priests and brides, New England house
and sand, of altar cloth and bed,
imagined space and dreamed-of god,
of woman, book, bones, fields at night,
a fence, or gold-caparisoned horse.

But on this sea, in this blank morning of our year,
with this wild leader in his wild pursuit,
this color without color locks us in
a palsy, new-found fear.
This white that stares me in the face
looks at me like a dusted enemy more fierce
than Ahab or than death:
a snow, disease, like leper's scales, teeth
that crumble at a touch yet tear
like no known beast.
What thing creates this air?

The world this morning is awry.
That captain should be one to tell me why
nature so suddenly lies out,
a broken mirror, to reveal
(white wheel in broken wheel)
herself cosmeticked like a whore.
But he, look, his eyes are on himself, or,
darkened from the night of his intent, we
fall upon this whiteness like a shore, where
bones and scum and wood and sand
leave us, eyeless, in a lipless jaw!

Ahab's movements and sounds have been mere stirrings and
mutterings. But now that he knows his crew is awake, he
breaks, pivots a half circle and confronts Ishmael with the same
pose and look in which he has, up to now, confronted the
powers of the air. Ishmael cowers, for what he sees is a devil
mask, a grinning god. On Ahab's face is written his double
purpose. He is both a warrior prepared for battle and a shaman,
ready, by tricks of incantation, to excite other warriors to the
battle. He towers high over Ishmael like an Aztec figure, a
Huitzilopochtli, and Ishmael cannot endure the sight. He drops
back before him, down on one knee.

But it is precisely on Ishmael that Ahab intends to advance, precisely to him that he intends to dance. To achieve the end he has now in mind, he knows he cannot command Ishmael so much as he must awe him. Before he can order Ishmael to do the thing he wants he must woo him first. So, no matter how he waves the harpoon as a wand to invoke the enemy, the White Whale, or uses it over Ishmael with the mock reverence of a Cross, Ahab must be a bridegroom-devil, as well as a shaman-priest, to work Ishmael to the proper pitch.

He therefore starts his BLACK EUCHARIST DANCE massively, calmly, with the deliberateness of the Mass. After he has given Ishmael the chance to see him as he is, he thrusts the harpoon, still held in the middle by both hands, out and up from him, and, with that movement of presentation, begins. He moves down and around Ishmael as a priest crisscrosses an altar, now holding the harpoon by its iron head with his hands cupped holy-like as though it were a chalice, now shaking it like a censer over Ishmael's head.

When he thinks he has Ishmael led near enough to the gate of superstition he begins to free his movements. Ishmael rises, and Ahab, using the harpoon to make his points, dances *his* answer to Ishmael's opening questions. The fearful whiteness is not *his* doing, it issues from the malice of the White Whale, and Ishmael, no less than Ahab, can only escape from it by doing battle with the Whale itself. Terror is only slain in the very jaw of terror, is the conclusion Ahab works to force Ishmael to.

At the moment that Ahab feels he has made this point on uneasy Ishmael, he breaks the iron head out of the shaft and, with typical high scorn and show, casting off his subtleties, presents the iron, barb down and cup up, like a revelation. Ishmael, fixed and fascinated, stands frozen to his will and, when Ahab speaks out, low and sure, in a hiss

Your blood, Ishmael, your blood!

Ishmael nods without knowing why. Then Ahab, captain enough to drive any of his crew when he has them heated to his proper temperature, quickly inverts the harpoon head again, with the barb end cuts Ishmael's arm, holds the cup of it swiftly under to catch the blood, forces Ishmael down to his knees, and, raising the harpoon up before him, cries out:

EGO NON BAPTIZO TE IN NOMINE PATRIS SED IN NOMINE
    DIABOLI!

And when Ahab breaks off the spell at his will, Ishmael moves after him, tranced, a servitor. As they go to the whaleboat together to do the final thing before the "battle," to prepare the coil of rope to which the harpoon must be attached, they both keep a flush of excitement on them, some of it a reflection of the "baptism" they have just been through, most of it the hither knowledge that the White Whale is near. Ahab is fully captain, there is a mastery about him, if for no other reason than that the chase is on him; Ishmael is most the obedient seaman committed at last by the force of Ahab's black act but lifted too by the chase.

At the boat Ahab indicates that he wants to double his line to make doubly certain of the enemy. Ishmael goes off and returns quickly drawing after him on the deck the head of a line which continues to snake its way after him as he coils it in an auxiliary tub in the whaleboat.

Ahab fixes the barb back into the pole and stands in the center of his deck, the harpoon in his hand like a staff, overseeing the coiling of the rope, waiting for its end to come, in order that he may fix the harpoon to it. Occasionally he deigns to straighten out a loop in the line with his foot, occasionally a snarl with his free hand – a boss.

The two men are now bound together, now work together, now handle together the fatal line. Together thay wear a new fatality,

Ahab's different from Ishmael's, a fatality he has not shown
before. It is not Ishmael's young, still questioning plunge into
the waters of event, the son entering his majority, but the resig-
nation of a father who sees his end in some not quite clear way
the consequence of himself. He is prepared to go to it without
further fuss, if for no other reason than that his life has run out.
But they are both caught in this line they handle, in fact and
image, a line which will tear Ahab out of life and leave Ishmael,
by no more than the accident of his years, the orphan at the
end to tell the tale. In this mood they fall into speech together
as they work:

I

AHAB: ISHMAEL:

My iron, my line!   Our noose, our death?

O lonely life!   Turn back! Turn back!

This line my fate   You *are* your fate,
this iron my will   choose, still!

Who lifts this arm?   You, Ahab, you!

No, boy, no,   Woe, captain, woe
the act's decreed   on fate to feed!

II

AHAB: ISHMAEL:

Wind, boy, wind   A shroud, a shroud!

Weave, boy, weave   Your grave, your grave!

This line my snare   A snare, a snare!

to catch white whale!   Beware! Beware!

III

AHAB: ISHMAEL:

  I, I alone   Am nothing, leader

  Ahab, Ahab   straw, straw

  I'll use you all!   Destroy us, rather

  The Whale! the Whale!   You! you!

The looped end of the line comes to Ahab's hand and with it
Ahab drops his last lingering glance back at life and its questions.
As he fastens the harpoon and line together his tone changes
and he begins to heighten the antiphonal speech. He knows the
whale cry is coming.

IV

AHAB: ISHMAEL:

  You'll leap, my coil!   White Whale, White Whale!

  You'll strike, my fang!   O jaw   o death

  I'll kill, I'll kill   O shame   o man
                                o mouth, be still!

  Down, creature, down!   O crown, of crown!

  I'll follow you!   Mad wake, mad wake!

  Now! now!   No, captain,
  now! now!   no!

At which moment the CRY comes:

  There she blows! There she blows! Like a snow-hill in the
  air! The White Whale, it is the White Whale!

and with it the action leaps out of the interlude of speech like
the flight of an harpoon and under an excitement which runs

out to the final moment like a line burning through chocks and
round the loggerhead. Like a dervish Ahab dances the DANCE
OF THE HARPOON. It is a dumb show of what will follow once
he is in the whaleboat and on the sea. The harpoon is in his
hand as spear, as sword, as knife, the final killing instrument,
and Ahab dances as the killer. As he bursts and drives, he calls
out directions to Ishmael and the crew busy with the boat:

Stand by the braces!
Hard down the helm!
Boats! Boats!

and, as if the boat were ready and on the sea, he leaps into it
with his iron poised. Ishmael leaps in after him and crouches
astern. Both convey the actual rolling of the boat, the confusion
of directing it, the tumble and broil of an actual chase. Their
exclamations follow hard on one another:

AHAB:
Forehead to forehead I meet thee!

ISHMAEL:
Behold! he swims a mighty
mildness!
Repose! But swift!

AHAB:
There go flukes!

ISHMAEL:
Ay, go, whale! The mad fiend
himself
is after you!

AHAB:
Look, below, the jaw!

ISHMAEL:
It breeches!

AHAB:

  Ay, white whale, breech,
  breech your last to the sun!
  Thy hour and thy harpoon are
  at hand!

            ISHMAEL:

              No, Ahab, no!
              Your hour! your hour!

AHAB:

  Not mine! not mine!
  Hemp only, only hemp
  can kill me!

            ISHMAEL:

              Look, Ahab, the line!
              the *line*, Ahab!

AHAB:

  My brain, my brain,
  o stave my brain!

            ISHMAEL:

              It swims away! O Ahab, stop!
              It seeks you not!

AHAB:

  I grow blind, blind!
  Is it night?

            ISHMAEL:

              It is thou, thou
              who seekest him!

AHAB:

    Yes, YES, towards thee I roll
    thou all-destroying but unconquering whale!
    To the last I grapple with thee,
    from hell's heart I stab at thee,
    for hate's sake I spit my last breath out to thee!
    Thus, thus I give up the spear!

Ahab hurls the harpoon. He keeps the line taut as it runs out through his hand but suddenly, though his other hand is trying to keep the line coming from the tub from fouling, a loop of it appears to go around his head, in a second tightens around his neck, and, in a great flight and leap Ahab is snapped out of his boat out of sight and into the sea.

ISHMAEL stays crouched in the stern, huddled before this sudden horror, his face the tale. When Ahab has gone, he drops his head, and holds as he is for an instant. Then he rises, steps down from the boat to the deck, comes forward, and at the boat's bow, where the harpoon was, speaks the epilogue:

    So Ahab went, bent on his intent
    down the sea, torn by his own taut line
    into a quick eternity

    The whale before, he after
    bound each to the other, wound
    in hemp and ocean, shroud

    His hate his death, his rest
    where bones are, ships, squid
    where fish feed

    Men and life of no avail
    to self-destroying Ahab
    faced with the white, white whale!

THE EPILOGUE

A man's fate
                 how he abate
                               the negatives in his given:
parents, place, income, hate
                               neighbors, rulers, friends
these pluralities
                 a man's fatalities
                               with which, from child, he's riven.

His self the other
                 within a frame
                               that curious mixture called
his name: Ishmael   Ahab   Stephen   John

his only instrument
                 to serve a purpose
                               earn him fame.

He starts
                 pushed by a ball
                               itself pushed by another
endlessly back
                 in billiard series
                               to that long cue
from which life's play began
                               this man:
cell, god, fish, bird
                 breach birth mother

The push no accident
                 nor he (though all else be)
If power is in him
                 was in nature's feeble first long step

to make himself
                    identity.

He earns his fate
                    to that degree
                              he push against all limits, bounds
palpable, unknown
                    thrust up against him:

devils, wars, failures, notions, sounds.

He the hazard
                    and the faith
      desperation what he need
                              those limits to exceed:
      drive without ruth
                    rathe to destroy
his own squeezed shame
                    the unbelief.

There is no other way
                    no outside answer
no god on whom to fix a blame
                    no truth.
                              For good and evil sown together
make man himself his only weather.

To think to pitch on whale's white hump
                              the evil and the wrong
and thus dispose of fate—
                    here Ahab erred
                              and in that error failed
his hate!

TROILUS

A Mask

Troilus, Cressid, Diomed
and a Chorus: a Young Man and a Girl

Time: the present or the past

Place: a city and where a city was

The Mask opens on a scene which should be at once a thriving
city and a dead one, at once a small park in a city and a plain
sown to salt.

The suggestions of buildings should be simultaneously skyscrapers and burnt out ruins, ancient walls and towers
as much as modern structures.

The desired feeling is of a place
as enclosed as a city yet with such holes blown through it that
the perspectives of emptiness are declared.

The center of the action should be something that is both a well
and a fountain, or bubbler, overthrown, as though, in falling,
the trough had dug into the ground.

Cressid sits beside it, on its
lip, as the curtain goes up.

Throughout the Mask water continues
to come up in broken spurts and flows, acting as an atonic
accompaniment to the action. Here, at the start, it is as feeble as
a weak bubbler, or neglected fountain.

Troilus is seated on something which should be a broken col-
umn and a park bench upset.

He sits in the way a man sits when he is telling over to himself his own bewilderments.

Both Troilus and Cressid are clothed as abstractly as the stage. They are neither ancient nor modern. That they may become themselves later (or two like younger people) they each wear a mask of age, Cressid's the heavier and ashier, a worn woman of pleasure. Troilus' impersonalized, revealing some of the clarity he accomplished by visiting, as Cressid has not, the seventh sphere.

Forestage, each at a wing, sit a young man and woman, quite at their ease, unobtrusive, the Chorus, dressed as Troilus & Cressid, but gayer in color, and without masks.

TROILUS speaks:
I am Troilus   once known, now not so known   not known for what happened to me, though that which happened happens each day to other men.
She there, bundle of rags, is   was   Cressid.
We have come back, rather, we have never left this desolated place. Troy! Troy! that *was* a city!   She   that *was* a woman I   that *was* a man, I, Troilus, whom men have spoken of!
Cressid! Cressid who was   *is* an image (as much or more than Helen ever was) of woman, of the love of woman. Helen   brought
a city down, Troy down but Cressid, this Cressid, my Cressid brought love down.

CHORUS 1 (the man):
                           Love is a fallen thing
CHORUS 2 (the girl):
                           It is of love we sing.

Cressid stirs, scratches inside her rags. Her back is to the audience. She is hunched up, a crone.

At which point, THE FIRST DANCE. TROILUS begins it, standing up to throw off the thoughts he has voiced, but only succeeding in transposing them, for, adagio, he starts to dance the male conviction "Love is a fallen thing."

CHORUS 1, as young shadow of the older man, echoes the movements, the lyric breaking off, stuttering to stop at each try—of the body, of the mind, of the spirit—to express its desire, the phrasings of the dance shattering at their ends like sentences interrupted, kisses soured, thoughts beaten to ground by stupid response.

The two men beat up again and again but always have the sense they fall, the presence of some alien will too much for their wills. It tears off each impulse, each advance.

When they give up, or, rather, when for the moment they fall back to puzzle over it, the girl, CHORUS 2, takes up the dance, contrapunto. She seeks to lift up against the men's despair another word: "It is of love we sing." But she moves hesitantly, having to admit, as woman, the men's persuasion. The heavy presence of Cressid as well opposes her, for she has to allow that Cressid's experience seems, on the face of it, corrective to her young faith.

Yet she sticks to a confidence in her own estimate of love's integrity, her steps gathering expression as she goes. She dances in a wider arc than the men and includes Cressid in her action circle. With each return from upstage left (above the well where Cressid sits) she gains assurance in the face of Troilus and the youth.

CRESSID, who has slowly, grudgingly given the girl attention as she danced by upstage from her, rises finally and, with a painful first turn, first shows herself to the audience.

This moment should be most sustained, decay the mark of her externals, but

her damnation showing out some animal gain, and former grace
implicit in her. Her first movements carry dignity beneath the
heaviness of age.

The CRESSID DANCE which here begins (the girl still with her,
though now falling into the echo role as the young man with
Troilus earlier) is a telling over of what happened to her, love's
history, a dumb show of the classic Troilus-Cressid-Diomed
story which it is the purpose of this Mask to unfold.

As Cressid
warms to it, the girl gives out and returns to her place to watch
(as Troilus and Chorus 1 watch) the dance go on to a climax.

Note: (it may need accenting that both Troilus and Cressid
dance here with a deliberation their age and suffering make
necessary. But this should in no way limit the possibilities of
movement. We in the West have so lost the syllables of the
dance, the fingers and toes and grass-blade shiftings of the body,
that it may not be obvious that such dance as here imagined
taps sources of power in movement we very much need again to
know.

Suffering, such as this man and woman have been through,
can only come to expression so.

Chorus 1 and 2, as the young, should be freer in their movement, more legs and arms, contemporary, western, suggesting,
however, at the same time—by their juxtaposition each to their
equivalent—that they are also personifications of Troilus and
Cressid as young lovers, of Troy.

What is known of Trojan dance
(I am thinking of Homer's description of the dances of the
Phaeacians for Ulysses in Book 6 on) should form the base of
both movements, the older and the young, with our movement
cut in. Such composition is of the essence of this whole Mask,
love's root and branch, the tradition, the fall, the taking up
again.

But no joint dancing at this early stage. This is the introductory
dance, a sketching on the part of all four characters of themes
and problems yet to enter the action of the Mask.)

TROILUS, who has watched Cressid with double feeling, pain so
great he cannot follow her story consecutively but looks and
looks away, but memory also, in the later stages of her dance
eased some by memory of her as a girl, speaks out of this latter
half of sense when she goes down at the well:

> The sea was soft that day I first sat by her
> its blue   (as we talked)   that white of afternoon
> when sun is strong   (it came from west before us
> across the strait).
>
> She played with sand (whose gold the air usurped)
> hiding her shyness in what holes her longish fingers,
> narrow hands so gently, probing made
> in that small lap of beach between us which
> had now become the spinning earth for me.
>
> What struck me was the difference in her glance
> from other women's ways of measuring man:
> the deep of modesty from which the boldness sprang
> as though already life had made her one long bow
> to draw back stiffly, strongly to let go
> this arrow, she
>   her eyes the bow, the string, the arrow, all
>   weapon, impulsion, barb, recoil.

CHORUS 1 & 2 alternately and together, thus:

CHORUS 1   By the sea her arms
            2   (boughs)
            1   sang the leaves
            2   (her hands)

```
1 & 2   downward
        the sun
        the sands

1       He heard the tendrils
2       (lips)
1       he knew the kiss
2       (to be)
1 & 2   bud and sap of his
        green tree

2       That day the beach
1       ran gold beneath his thigh
1 & 2   that day he knew
1       this woman his predestined sky
```

CRESSID, who, when she ended her dance, had sat facing the audience but with her head dropped on her chest, her look lost in the folds of rags in her lap, speaks like a bitter chorus her thoughts apropos Troilus' speech

(Dry and slow, alum):

We add so much, pile dream on fact.
He talked (talks now) as if the senses act
some inch beyond desire, select
their object with intent to go
a distance more than appetite.

He dreams   dreamt always   took
the fact for light, refused
to leave sand, hand, his skin
particulars I craved

craved as girl curious to taste
attention, his more than an other's perhaps
because he did dream, talk

because it was the summer, he was brown,
I'd left the others in the town
and, long-limbed, relaxed, I wanted him to throw me down.

CHORUS 1 & 2 together, miming the action by indirection in a
dance forestage:

They talked, swam, waited for night,
let the day run out
with supper, friends,   M
danced. And when it was time   O
when the dark made easier   V
the exchange of tongues   E
(language was babble   M
      flesh spoke)   E
he thought he loved,   N
she knew her sure desire.   T

CHORUS 1 & 2 continue to dance after their mime and comment
on the first meeting of Troilus and Cressid is finished. It is as
though this present moment on the stage is their own first meeting, these 3000 years later. Perhaps the change from the earlier
mode had better be accomplished by a dropping of hand masks
which they have used up to now. And I'm not sure but what
some of the briskness of two moderns ought to be the mark of
their behavior once the masks are down. Definitely it ought to
be a city meeting, not, as the meeting of Troilus & Cressid on
the shore of the strait.

The dance should carry into abstract movement the faltering
of the introductory dance, a coarseness bred of our animalistic
notions of sex, the jerkiness. The great danger the choreography
will have to watch is a comic result. The clues to avoid it are, I
hope, in the speech of Troilus below. He voices it alongside
their dance.

TROILUS speaks, as double agent, by indirection commenting
on these two latter-day lovers at the same time that, in his own
mind, he is dwelling on what happened to his own love which
Cressid, in his mind, betrayed:

Love is not present now,
has flown
            is not a state so separate as we think
which men and women breed by kiss and glance
            no dance
outside the modes and figures of that trance,
the full intent

That love at least must live
is lie we practice to protect
what we inherit, breath,
unwilling to admit
the large wrongs bring
love also down to
death

Why should love live
when all that should enforce it fails
this side of meaning
                  tearing off
what love alone is key to, form,
that feature nature wore
before man turned her, woman, whore,
when matter stood so many objects clear
not use, delight the round of human year

Love is not love with end, with objects lost.
Means wither. Bodies, gestures fall.
                        All nature falls.
The path, are blown along the path, papers, dust,
cloth (strips which give no clue
dropped without care
picked up, lamely, at a dare)

The path, love is the path.
                              And, in the forest, calls, calls!
We shall answer, find.
But if love now is lust
or mere drift back
better we know and say
we do not know the way

The way, love is
the way!

In other words, the dance of CHORUS 1 & 2 should be a search
both for each other and for love, the stage a forest where they
meet and pass, unable to discover in each other, as Troilus and
Cressid did, some beginning. By "in the forest, calls, calls" they
should have exchanged the sides of the stage which they have
been associated with up to now and should there give up in
admission of their failure to find each other or the way, so that
Troilus' last lines are spoken without movement to distract
from them, the young man and the girl marking by their
positions the truth of what he says: "We do not know the way."

It is the close of what might be called Part One of the Mask.

AS OF TROILUS, the Anatomy of Love: biosis.

Troilus is, by and large, to be your own voice, to be the sufferer who tries, by turning over his own experience, to form a critique: ex. "Love is not present now." Yet, because he is inside his own tragedy, he cannot be allowed the objective statement.

Nor can Cressid, because she undid love. Yet, because she was harsher, she arrived at bases of love Troilus would never come to. Her lack of courage—"slidinge of courage"—I see as a carelessness, a despair, a sort of fatality arising from the very hotness and sharpness of her sensuality. It has to do (as compared to Troilus) with how much head sexuality gets in the field of sensuality. Troilus, on the other hand, is weighted on the sensuality side. Both are incomplete, and must, in the play, create the tragedy by their incompleteness.

The fact is, as now imagined, there does not seem to be a role from which the completeness can be seen. Chorus 1 & 2 are observers, but, imagined as the modern young, they are searchers, know no conclusions, and, at the end, have only the gain of having observed the Troilus and Cressid story. Their only gain over the audience is the fact they are participants as well.

Diomed must be a Kulikowski:* all sword, full sexuality, and what is sensual only the accident of sex. He should be active, active, and this his attraction to Cressid, and to Troilus who, in his duel with him, is defeated from the first.

BUT WHERE THE TRUE CHORUS? Can it be allowed to reside in me as creator, as echo rather than voiced? Or should the play be given another chorus, a narrator one step beyond the Chori? And what is the position of said true chorus?

---

*Adam Kulikowski, a friend of the poet; Polish emigré and editor of *Opportunity*, a magazine for businessmen. See also Olson's poem for him entitled "For K," which begins "Sex the sword . . . ." Ed.

no data	1	Love is not present now
hypothesis	2	Imagination or illusion as container: again Troilus has it, especially in his seventh sphere scene
gravitation	3	The morality of physics: the body as flux, as Browning movement, as pool of isotopic, metabolic ingredients: the whole position of man in the gravitational field
	4	Bogomolets,* and the time scheme of a human life: the clash of two rhythms, nature's and man's
research		THE STORY: read, first, Benoît de Ste.-Maure's *Roman de Troie* (ll. 13065-21782), Guido delle Colonne's *Historia Trojana,* Boccaccio's *Filostrato* (Philadelphia: 1929, translation by Griffin and Myrick), Lydgate's *History, Sege, and Destruccion of Troy,* Caxton's *Recuyell of the Historyes of Troy**
		THE MATERIAL: Stendhal, de Gourmont, Kwanami and Seami's *Komachi,* Henryson's *Cresseid,* Shakespeare's *Troilus and Cressida*

---

*Alexander A. Bogomolets (1881-1946), president of the Ukrainian Academy of Science and director of the Institute of Experimental Biology and Pathology at Kiev. See esp. his *The Prolongation of Life* (New York: 1946). Ed.

**Sources mentioned in F. N. Robinson's edition of Chaucer (Boston, 1933). Ed.

CABEZA DE VACA

An idea for an opera

There are two chief voices, that of a woman, and of the man Cabeza. The other voices are

brown song: another woman, of the Islands, and a fierce, froward male voice, the Conquistador (Cabeza's grandfather, from whom Cabeza recoils). ((From the two women Cabeza learns what he shall find out how to practice.))

1st white song: (such shall constitute narrative passages as well as the running reaction of Cabeza to his experience; so, with the Woman, it will be both soliloquy & dialogue, the Woman chief narrator and the man sometimes going on the sound track of his thoughts)

the 1st white song, then, is: the passage of, the Ocean

red song: what is met, a thing of which Cabeza has knowledge through brown song, yet which, in meeting him (due to such as his Grandfather who came first), meets him harsh, strong, & enslaves him for seven years

my impression is, here is a place for chorus, yet, for skeleton production the dependence of the text and music can be on two voices, a man and a woman, so that, in

(a) *the meeting*

(b) *the enslavement*

(c) *the trust*

& (d) *the emergence*

the two red voices (male & female) and the two
white voices are working in and out of each other

blacksong is now finally heard strong, though, in the music, it
should well have existed in 1st white song, and to have come
stronger behind 1st red song, all through the central pain
                                                                    *black-
song* is a man, a man more like Cabeza than the idea of black
and white would suggest, a man of alertness but of a tendency
to exaggerate wonder in the direction of the superstitious & the
false magical, whereas Cabeza, with no loss of confidence in the
wonder of life as its power (thus Cabeza is healer extraordinary,
in the next section), does not lose what the Woman keeps
reinforcing, that the act of magic is the true oppose to the act
of logic (from which comes Grandfather, & all blind white
mice)

> *blacksong* is companion, walks west all black beside
> Cabeza all white in doeskin, the two of them singing
> like apple trees blowing, & throwing, seeds, and
> flowerings, a wondrous singing of the beauty of
> things and of man alive in the phenomenal world (in
> which the Indians join, also walking, and behind
> which, in a sort of triumph, sounds the Woman; so
> here, *allsong*, walking

suddenly broken by one of the Indians falling, in pain, gripped
by *Bad Thing*

> Bad Thing is no person but a voice, which stops all,
> and is a voice of an order different from anything
> which has been heard though with one mnemonic,

the Grandfather, though the Grandfather pitched and
freed from such material greed; this greed is what
plays on men, anywhere, what eats us

> literally: Indian

says, Bad Thing came in the night and ate part of his
inside

and so, the action is Cabeza's healing of,
the terror; and the song is the song of *the hand*
as love and *the voice* (with Cabeza's hand on the
Indian) the act of *recognition*, the teaching that the
only endurances are structures of activity (what,
properly, the white song may be said to be able to
add to red song, brown song, black, the only *proper*
individualism)

THE END, is a splitting of this force in two directions:

> first,

blacksong leads other whites back to redsong, but, because of
the false thing in black *without* white, the white men black
leads are the archetype of Grandfather, and two things
happen:

the Indians kill Stephen as he tries to run away, misunder-
standing their hospitality

and then the Whites fall on and kill all Indians

Cabeza stumbles, though he is somewhere else (perhaps, here,
it is possible to have two stages, or a division of the stage, so
that Woman observes both actions

> Cabeza, though now in full

power of practice (his triumphant song of healing sounding
still), is surrounded by whites, disengaged from the brown
and the red, and is overborne by the mass will to destroy:
greed (Grandfather) is too strong, and Cabeza goes under, not

so much killed as defeated

                and the voice at the end is Woman,
holding the vision, sounding it at the end, yet, by coda of all
that is against vision, recognizing the nature of the defeat

-------------------------------- * * * * *--------------------------------

documentation: brown song: Canary Islands

                   white song: double, Cabeza the tradition, the
                                    Woman the tradition plus *gener-*
                                    ative materials

                   black song: high Negro, that is, Kabyl or
                                    North African mountain sources

                   redsong: American Indian instrumentation
                                    & scale

principle of counterpoint: the relevance of the *conservative* &
the *generative*

THE BORN DANCER

A Ballet

people: Nijinsky ([Tim] LaFarge)

Diaghilev ([Wesley] Huss? or some hombre
        larger than LaFarge)

Romola (Betty [Jennerjahn])

The Russian Officer ([Victor] Kalos)

Kyra (one of the new girls, the tall ones,
        almost LaFarge's height — & male feet
        and ankles)

ACT I

dance #1—Nijinsky enters, in exploding leap, *down* and out, as if
    from the hand of god, or the palm of nature.

The job: to make convincing, the huge *original*
(animal, sensual, metempsychotic) power of the
human body as it is innately, practically wild, without indifference, but wholly self (assured, empowered,
whatever—almost blind, it goes

                         at the same time, to
get in, that this is not what we associate with any of
the above adjectives, in that there is no separation
whatsoever from the highest human content—this
thing is informed by rhythm with intellection, soul &
will, even though each are, here, at this starting, like
the Gray Slave of it, the above, innate, still not
wandered around in by Nijinsky himself

it is the dance of man as born god because he is child
of nature in the full sense of planets as well as plants

> (*notes for Tim:* get Katy [Litz] to dance for
> you her memory of the roles of (1) Spectre de
> la Rose, (2) the Gray Slave, (3) Petrouchka
>
> and you yourself study all photographs of
> Nijinsky as same, make-up, posture, etc)

dance #2—Diaghilev & Nijinsky (Diaghilev to Nijinsky's left
throughout, at first adding to Nijinsky's powers, and
seeming to be equal to Nijinsky (Nijinsky even thinking himself smaller, but, his power, equaling
Diaghilev's dimension

> the job here (choreographically) is to so construct the
> movement of Diaghilev, and of the two together, that
> Diaghilev seems to become more and more rising wall,
> on Nijinsky's left, until, at the end of the dance, he
> is straight and almost so overtopping that he leans
> center stage above the withering figure of Nijinsky:
>> Diaghilev is power as the world is power,
>> know-how (very much like Lincoln Kirstein!
>> in looks! I would even help you make a mask
>> for Diaghilev to look like beetling Lincoln in a
>> pea jacket!); and male-raper—sensual in the
>> sexual sense, due to no center, no intimate
>> center innate as Nijinsky has, only, at center,
>> a small fist of greed for pleasure and world
>> power; and so, for young Nijinsky, a hammer
>> by which he is pounded down on so
>>
>> Nijinsky is, in this first encounter with that
>> other reality—the consciously selected, which,
>> by fist alone, deceives itself (or others are

deceived to think it) has mastered the natural unselectedness of, "life," eh?—*enclosed,* tightened, scared (Nijinsky's innocence is not yet possessed of any consciousness and so is somewhat easily beaten down

the dance, dance #2, is *imprisonment #1*

dance #3 — *Romola — Nijinsky — Diaghilev*

Romola comes up from Nijinsky's right, and Nijinsky uses her to offset Diaghilev, trying, by her, to create a polar tension on which he can (still innocent, especially of any sexual action other than that which his own movement as dancer contains) tight-walk his way out of—away from—Wall #1

at first, of course, there is some new play (fresh movement, choreographically) in Nijinsky, and it is lyric (the opposite of the Spectre sexuality, the hermaphroditic, which should be strong in dance #1— Nijinsky, there, is man *and* woman, or man-woman-child, undifferentiated sex, huge original Morphodite, the Double-Backed Beast):

here, as against #1, which splits off first in #2 as homosexual, splits off now as normal male

(*though*, warning, Tim, always, Nijinsky's sensuality or sexuality is played against the larger, innate, innocent-wise fuller purpose of "life" as force —which neither Diaghilev nor Romola, then, or ever, can know)

in the middle, Diaghilev withdraws, defeated, but in the end, after Romola and Nijinsky have had their fling, Nijinsky is left in the same condition as with

Diaghilev: Romola becomes Wall #2, and again he is
smaller than the enemy!

dance #4 (end of Act I)

Nijinsky & the Insane Asylum

no person for the Insane Asylum—the Third Wall is,
the space ahead of Nijinsky, in other words, between
him & his audience, which, he is to dance before,
toward, and finally against, as he has, ditto, to the
left Nijinsky, to the right Romola

it is the Wall as all things—and the pattern of the
choreography classically repeats (but with all the
variation you can muster) the kinetic of dances 2 & 3

—that is, at first, the Wall of
his own first large consciousness (he is now—what?—
25, is the father of Kyra, has worked with such men
as Picasso, Massine, whoever Stravinsky—and is more
knowing (in fact more knowing, in the true sense,
than any of them!) is exciting, does for him, in its
own form, what Diaghilev and then Romola did, at
first

but by like token (that he is
confronted by the very given of his birth which
makes him the thing he is—the Rimbaud of the twen-
tieth century) he here too goes under

and the Insane Asylum (the veil between him and the
audience) raises itself, finally, as Wall #3—and he is
left, at the end of Act I, a sort of Petrouchka heap,
on the floor

ACT II

the hardest job of all, Nijinsky alone, in the box Act I
leaves him in, walled, but, working, working, doing
what his *Diary* is the tale of, working through

watch
any temptation to do all the foolish things everyone
has done with him in this period, even to the point
where his drawings have been turned into mandalas to
examine his insanity!

it is true, they clearly establish
that he was insane, but this, surely, is the smallest
part of the story, and should only be used as the
natural issue of what the tearing of his tissue by
Diaghilev and Romola caused—and the natural split-
second insanities that any man of such power is heir
to

but the dance, this dance, you must contrive from
the full text of the *Diary,* the perceptions therein—
which are of such an order that I confidently call him
a second Rimbaud

the story should be the Victory of, Metempsychotic
(not Psychotic) Man over humanism—the return of
Nijinsky to the state of Dance #1, but, now, so many
years and experiences later, thicker, slower (that is, as
against the crouchings and the speeds of #1

one should be leading, at the end of Act II, to the
feeling, that if all idiots, including his keepers
(Diaghilev & Romola) were removed, this man, this
man-god, no longer child, could DANCE like he or
man has never danced

but, at the end, there is no such possibility: he is like
an arrow, a huge arrow, standing up straight, huge,
from the bow of the stage, now, finally, again, ALONE
—his dimension towering over the not-present
Diaghilev and Romola and Insane Asylum Wall—but
unable to move

(*note*: Tim, if you can end this like a sudden poised
abrupt motionlessness, you will have done an extraordinary thing—the real issue of, the *Diary*)

ACT III

very swift, like an epilogue, but, returning, the second
take, the ultimate re-take of Dance #1

    it opens with Kyra leading Nijinsky along
some path, say, through woods

    (Kyra is almost identical with Nijinsky—almost is
    like his twin, as he was in Dance #1. In fact, here,
    you should let Kyra be the coda of Dance #1,
    especially, when he does burst, she is like a shadow
    dancing off from him, but, in the audience's eye, as
    reminder, sign, of what it is to have done what
    Nijinsky now does

the provocation is, the Russian Officer, who is to
stand, on your stage, for all his troop, whom the
Nijinskys come up on, in the forest. They take him
and Kyra first as nothing but other Displaced Persons,
as, in truth, they are—why Nijinsky is out of the
Insane Asylum. They give him drink, after food. He
begins to sharpen. They recognize who he is. They
plague him to dance (as people might ask a child to
play the piano). He knows what they are after. He is
rusty, oldish, scared, reluctant to take up what has
been so long unused—in fact, what he himself has
gone beyond or, forgotten. But the drink, and the
fire, and the pull of the Russian Officer, who pulls
him in a sort of a way like Diaghilev and Romola did,
earlier—as Kyra never does, because she, alone, is of
his flesh—that is, he is pulled, as any such man is, by

another human life. So he does it. He starts, and, from pain, it comes, all the way, until, you shall dance beyond what Act II is, you shall dance as Shiva might, say. Until, at the end, how I don't know, it is as though he shot straight *up* into the air.

CURTAIN

APOLLONIUS OF TYANA

A Dance, with Some Words, for Two Actors

The dancer, APOLLONIUS
The voice, TYANA, or place

The Introduction, or
THE GAMBIT

Some light should come on, before the first words of the introduction are spoken, but it should be small light, and slow over the general area, only enough to decrease the original blackness to the condition of shadow among rocks or in a mountain pass when the day is off west. A very white stick of light then picks out from the general obscurity a hump about two-thirds of the way back on an oblique axis from the audience. It is the two actors, sitting on the floor faces front, the dancer close inside the legs of Tyana, so close as to obscure the body and head of the other actor.

As Tyana speaks the introduction most slowly and most clearly, it should be as though the words came out of the mouth of the forward figure, the dancer—whose lips do not move, or his features, at first, they are held, and it is like a soliloquy in the cinema, with the face steady and the words coming from the sound track, like thoughts alongside the concentration.

As the introduction proceeds, however, the dancer should discover movement, first of his face, then of his fingers, until the most dramatic discovery for him is his two arms. And when he raises them out and to the side, Tyana, too, should accompany him, so that, at a high moment, they compose together a four armed figure.

As the introduction comes to its ending, a two armed, two legged man is erect, the single dancer himself, ready to move

57

off, to make his next discoveries in space. (There is no reason
why, for a split second, timed to the content of the speech, he
should not be the classic proportional figure of man, bound by
a circle, legs and arms spread to cut the circle into four arcs—a
sudden geometric and annunciative man measurer and to be
measured.

As and when Apollonius moves off, Tyana swings to an easy
reclining position, indolent, you might say, lying like a confi-
dent thing, on one elbow, and watching all movements of the
dancer, constantly pushing and pulling the dancer away and
towards herself, by traction, through concentration. And there
will be moments when Tyana will fall back, as though into
sleep, leaving Apollonius free, leaving all attention solely on the
dance.)

TYANA:

It is not remembered that three of the chief of men
were born pretty much at the same time: Buddha, Confucius,
Lao-Tze, three places three men, three of men who were not
content with what had been, who found it necessary to shape
themselves with greater accuracy than had been men's wont, at
least in their time, to try to make more sense out of experience
than ambience alone ever allows.

Let me detach your minds from religion. Let me, instead,
direct your minds to birth, how men, once born, seek to be
born another way—and without necessary reference to such
words as "spirit" or "the after-life." In other words, let me
remind you that men, first, deal with their lives, their discoveries therein—in their own and other lives—and that they seek by
their actions, if they are serious men, to concentrate their own
and others' attentions to the closer intervals, not of any removed place but of the intervals which surround us here, here in
the distraction of the present and the obvious, in short, that
which surrounds us, what we make, what we live in and by and

(not so often) for—as such as these did live, as such as he lived
whom I want here to tell you most about, a man whom here
and now I am offering to you anew.

His name is mostly forgotten. But there are reasons, political
reasons that, since the 3rd century of the Christian era, since
the Empress Domna Julia wanted to know more about him, no
one has heard much about him, even though there was a time
when he was as known as his twin, that twin you well know,
whom I, in fact, because I am a Cappadocian, would say you
know too well, too little and too well, one Jesus Christ.

I wish you only to note how men spring up, when they are
needed, like violets, on all sides, in the spring, when the winter
has been too long. 500 years after Buddha, Confucius, Lao-Tze,
two men sprang up: the Christ, to honor him as you do, and
this man, to whom I now call your attention. They were born
very close to the same time and not so very far apart in space
(in space, that thing which means so much to me as a force,
more than it does seem to mean to you) 500 air miles, say—like
you say, so easily—north north east of where Christ was born;
and in an area mostly now forgotten or thought of as where
Turks are or some other dark-skinned people who peddle rugs,
or better, pieces of carpet, and have round spots on their cheeks
like vaccinations.

It is curious about ignorance, how it thrives—even ignorance
of such a common thing, such an easily found out thing as the
contours and peoples of what any of us share, the earth. Or
ignorance, for that matter, of time—what has gone on in time
amongst others as well as yourselves, you who have quarrelled
largely, have moved from civil war of farming brothers to civil
war of all of us—and for what? for peace, for petroleum, the
newest silly sediment.

But there you are. Even your newest war of the world comes
home to me, comes to me the center of what was anciently the
world and is now again—and just in such terms as resources

and war—the center of the world. But I am a Cappadocian and
as a child of the Caucasus Mountains (as you all, actually, are),
I do not propose to offer anything but what you used to be able
to deal with so firmly: facts. It is time now, as it always is, to
put aside ambiguities. I shall not let issue from myself by one
hair or fissure of myself the slightest ambiguity, any double
talk. For you are not here for riddles. The answer, in fact, is
always, was always, the simplest, even though it may, for so
many, stay riddle. If there is any truth at all, it is only you
yourself, you who was born on four legs, who found out how
to walk on two and who would wish—who hopes—so to manage
his strength that he will stay erect, will not have to come down
to end as we all began, almost on all fours. At least you will try
to avoid being so forced down hill that you will not have to, like
some Australian creature, go to the grave on three.

How shall you manage it? You see, ascension is an invention.
Gotama Buddha, one day, lay down to die, and after telling his
closest friends, and those flies his disciples, that he was about to
die, they, pressing on him for some final message, the fools,
heard what any wise man should remind his fellows: that they,
too, had work to do to shape themselves before they too died as
he was dying, and that that shape they only could fashion, out
of themselves, that he was no more than a man who had spent
his time doing his fashioning, that was all. In other words, the
tale I have to tell has a beginning and an end.

So let us begin. Let me show you something of this man of
my own place, something remarkable on him like a coast has
things which stand out like a white house or a clump of trees,
some such thing which has not heretofore been revealed of this
man who moved off from me, from Tyana where he was born,
who moved most gradually from this center out as far as a man
then could go

                            and does it matter how far, so long as
it is far, as far as any particular man can go?

can you say how far far is? can you
think of any man of all these I have mentioned who (except
for Gotama, perhaps) moved as far as you shall see this man
move, as far as, indeed, so far as space goes, as you too have the
opportunity to move

do you recall that even Kung Fu Tse
had not, he admitted, been as far as Tai, the precious mountain?

and certainly you do know how local
Christ was.

There are two things to be said about this Apollonius of
mine, of Tyana, two things he was most aware of, more aware
of, certainly, than any one but one other man, perhaps, in all
the time since, of all the men who have been busy, in that time,
about human business.

I don't mean to press you too hard. Let me be quiet and direct. I want you only to recognize that far is not so very far,
and that my lad, this Apollonius knew, as I say, two important
things: ONE, that how is it far if you think of it, but, TWO, that
far could not well be less than that you think of it yet it must
be more and that to find out how more one must MOVE.

And so he moved, off from me,
he moved as only, before him, from my mountains, the race
moved, Buddha moved, and since, man has—well, he has mi-
grated but still, who, among you, has so moved?

MOVE one

Apollonius moves, as slowly as he discovered his limbs, off
gradually to stage left, in other words south south west, to
ANTIOCH. And when he does arrive at this first limit, the lighting should define the whole segment of that geography, in a
color special to itself and the wall of the color abrupt, like a
jigsaw slice—in order that each of the moves to follow shall add

themselves by the action of Apollonius' dance until the whole
stage area is transformed into the ancient world, from India to
Cadiz, a colored "map" of it, with the Mediterranean the axis,
and that axis oblique to the audience, in other words running
from upper stage left to lower stage right. If possible the colors
should come on as outlines of coasts simultaneously with
Apollonius' movements as those movements define those coasts
or, where it is inland, new topographies—in other words, the
feeling, both of the movement of the man and the color should
be the creation both of periploi (charts of coasts) and of topo-
graphical maps.

TYANA:

He left me, first, for Antioch: a man cannot abide for long
the place of his birth, the place of his first experience, the thing
is too close for him to know, not what it is, but how to gauge it.
And besides, there is the body, the physical thing, it has to be
explored. For in what sense is it not the base of the legend?
And yet is it not, strangely, what we know least about, this
huge earth we know less about than we even know of the other,
the larger one? of these mountains of kidneys which can suddenly crumble, of this Great Lakes of the liver, of this Tigris
and Euphrates system the heart, which can so easily break and
then there is death, of these Neocene bones, the geology of ourselves, which live longest, of this seed and strange cotyledon,
the brain, of these flowers and grasses which can be cut off, the
fingers? What do we guess of our own functions and of their
most private life, their dangers—despite all our speculation
about arrowheads, or storms in nebulae, or whether Africa or
Asia was where an ape got the use of his thumb, or the use of
fire?

The thing is, Apollonius was interested, 1st, that when man
invented a city he got important (so far as we, the children of
cities are concerned) and 2nd, that healing, any kind of healing,

like any kind of usable discovery, starts with the human body, its complicated and animal structure, what the masters he first went to understood to rest in *kinesis*.

The dance of Antioch is *the dance of the body*, and the body as first part of the way. His masters were of the Aesculapian-Pythagorean school, and had drawn out of the ancient world disciplines for the body and its health which rested on the concept that to heal it is necessary first to know, and that to know is more than mechanics, however much any knowing of the body must rest on a complete knowledge of its behavior. It is a concept we have only known the ragged end of, and so we have doctors for the mind and doctors for the body and neither of them know what a dancer now has to know, or a composer, or a poet, if any of these latter craftsmen are honestly attacking their craft.

What Apollonius was first taught was, that how a tree sways is as much of the matter as is how you sway; how any hanging thing is as you hang by the hook of gravitation, hang, as a pendulum swings: how, to heal, is also how you eat and how you find out how—somehow—to maintain your resistance (of which act secrecy is an honest part, his Pythagorean teachers taught him).

And he said, Apollonius said, it was his conclusion, that what he got from Antioch was, how to act fiercely but, with dignity.

And he ate no animal food and he wore nothing made of animal skin. Blood seemed to him of consequence. His feeling was, that man has no right to use anything but what, like a crop or the wool of a sheep, can grow again—like trees can grow, if top soil is not the price paid for cutting a stand off, as war cuts off men after their mothers can bear again

APOLLONIUS speaks:

How do you differ yourselves from how you eat, eh? How do you

make a god (which is the same as how do you make an image
of yourself) without making him all maw, as you yourselves
are, with your body unknown and merely set off, like an
eating machine, by some button, as you set war off?

How
are you anything but a hole in the earth?

And he moved on.

MOVE two

First, he returned home, to Tyana. His father had died, and left
him and his brother the family wealth. Apollonius resigned his
share of the patrimony. It was not difficult for him. He put it
very quietly. He said,

> I give it away to those who desire such
> things. Naked I seek the Naked.

It was no more and no less a decision than Gotama's, the only
difference, obviously, that Apollonius did not have such a
struggle over the world. Perhaps, as it is now, the world was not
so attractive, and the decision was easier than it was for Gotama
who had a white horse and such a handsome wife and child.

When Apollonius moved off again, he went south south east,
down the two old rivers of the East, to BAGDAD. We have forgotten what any Arab knows, that Bagdad, for all the long years
—the centuries—after the collapse of man's first disciplines
(man's first cities), Bagdad remained the intellectual center, the
old intellectual center, and much more in touch with the nerve
ends of the old path than Alexandria ever was, or than the
newest Alexandria, your Manhattan is, today, any clue to the
path, the path which doesn't die, the path which is no more
than yourself, if you can find it.

Apollonius did a natural thing,
to start to find it, but not an easy thing, especially for a gregar-

ious man. And surely Apollonius was no monk, as you shall discover, was no thin fellow without a roar in his chest. He was no bull, that is also true, but he was loaded with an appetite for the real world, the world we forget is the world as we love it—the world of other men. He craved to talk, as any live man does, to get at things by talking about them. In fact, he was one of those who talked to live. But he came quickly on a danger: that it is not easy to keep talk from sliding into small talk and at the same time it is not easy for talk to avoid (in order to avoid small talk) parables, anecdotes, all those easy stoppages of conversation which pass themselves off as wisdom sayings and are nothing more than schmerz, than, ah, how large life is and how long, which doesn't matter a breath to any live man, how his predecessors were eternal about it, it does not matter, he only wants to be sharp about it, to stay on its point, to hold all that it contains, not dissipate an ounce of it by any such gener-alizations, however couched in humor or weh. So Apollonius took a vow of silence for five years. He put this burden on himself, this bit. He said not one thing for five years. He lis-tened, instead. He found out how to hear. He stripped himself of the heartiest thing of all, next to passion: he stopped the lively little animal, his tongue. He made his breath stay home. He wore his mind as firmly as, at Antioch, he had found out how to wear his body.

You can call it a descent, a sinking down into—as a poet, say, sinks—into (it is not easy to say what it is one sinks into) but it is surely clear what a blind place it is, and yet how, it is wholly related to light, to that which we identify with the light of the mind. The mind also has kinesis, and a large part of its behav-iors are, like the body's, matters of struts and strains, and they take examination that speech, too easy a speech, loses the voice of, loses the body and breath of. So, again, he was an alert man, to take silence on while he mastered the things of the mind Bagdad had to offer him (the more overtly intellectual things—

like languages, or engineering—in contrast to the geometry, the more hermetic knowledge he had before, of the Pythagoreans).

The dance, then, here in the gray and gold light of the FIRST VALLEY, is *the dance of the mind as mute*—muted man and muted place: Tyana sits with her eyes and ears wide open (so Apollonius dances) but with a marvellous warmth and openness to the silent mouth (the mouth become as lips are which have the beauty of kiss—with no rattling, there, of the white teeth, those busy horses). Both actors should achieve, around their mouths, this richness which nobody knows any more, of how a river looks which moves winningly and doesn't say a word, of how eyes are when the mind is clearly a clear thing and only doesn't speak its content because it knows what apothegms never quite get across—that however tragic is experience, it is altogether beautiful, just in itself, however difficult it is

> to check winds, waves, and the inroads
> of vermin and of beasts
>
> a middle term, as it were,
> between gods and men

(It is *Apollonius speaking*, for the first time, after five years)

> And at Babylon
> I was not satisfied with the four golden eggs
> hanging from the roof of the Magi's hall
> which they said, were the tongues of gods
> and were wheels with wings, or spheres,
> vaguely associated with fate

Tyana takes it up: For he
> was not one to settle at all
> for sacred or magic objects in the places of
> that telesma he had his eye on, how
> consecrated a man can make
> himself

Apollonius: How can I find out how
to be so resistant that
I make wrong things fly off,
go off, where they belong,
which is where nothing is

Tyana: There are no four eggs,
or two, there is no image
or symbol adequate
to that which is going on . . .

Apollonius: . . . because I am going on

Tyana: It ought to be enough if his action
is adequate to drive off beasts,
and all carelessness: the idle only
are nothing

Apollonius: And it is from them alone that all manipulators
buy their food: plasma
of the animal, human or otherwise, and that juice
all witch men, high or low, feed off, the white stuff
—none of it, no superstition, animal or magical
equals
the job in hand

Tyana: And how can I teach him
his hands?

MOVE three

For more clue, Apollonius went, this time, West, straight into
the Mediterranean world. The dance, and the dancer, now really
travel. The movement, and the coming of the colors, are much
freer, for with the sheaf of his mind and body bound, Apollonius is more open, welcomes place and persons more than his
previous preparations allowed for. He is less priggish, intense in

another way, without necessity of argument, and with much
more excitement to variants, all variations, of countries and of
peoples. He takes on the known world, with no nervousness,
and with a first assurance that he has a warm mind, however
sharp it is, that the heart and the mind are not enemies, are,
instead, twins (as the legs are), that motion depends on their
functioning together. So he is in no danger (as his world was) of
any superstition: he is on the lookout for man, and he is already
this side of Caesarism or Christism, has found out that either of
these dividings falls into ugly halves—of materialism or immortalism. He knows, as he moves through Alexandria, Athens,
Rome, Cadiz, that *his* job, at least, is to find out how to inform
all people how best they can stick to the instant, which is both
temporal and intense, which is both shape and law.

                But one thing he does not know—
the words and acts to pass to people so that they may instantly
recognize how to avoid both Caesarism and Christism. In lieu of
yet knowing a methodology, he looks for it—he looks into
everything, politics, art, whore-houses, churches, stores, people
sitting in the square at evening, lovers, marriages, idiots, emperors, ravening birds as well as blowflies, eating flowers, seamen,
great ladies, beaches where only mangrove precedes him, but
always cities, and men thick and single, always, where men are,
where they are making ports or new principal streets, how they
get crops in to the metropolises, how rich and poor farmers are,
how well or not well painters paint, how bad drama is now that
there is no Sophocles (who, as he himself is faithful, had been
faithful to the doctrines of the healer, Aesculapius). For in a
strange way drama is the objectification which has died out of
his world and which (in some way he is not yet clear about) is
joined to the very objectification (on all other planes of action)
which he is so very sure is called for, what he is after, in order
to enable man to assert his native harmonics, if man is to be
based, once again, wherever he is, on force and dignity.

It is the center of the dance-play, this *dance of the world,* this move across all the Mediterranean, and it is to be imagined, by the dancer, in this way: the world of the 1st century AD which Apollonius moves through is already the dispersed thing the West has been since, and through it wanders this other kind of man who somehow or other is not satisfied that the progress, the pushing out, the activity (of Rome pushing into Europe, or Cadiz pushing into the Atlantic), all the expanding of the earth or the heavens (even into Heaven) is worth a thing, is worth a penny more than what he had already, at 20, turned over to his brother.

Yet Apollonius does not know what, for certain, the Naked is which he feels himself turning on, and so, because he does not know, he holds tenaciously to what's before him, to what's in front of his eyes, or in the reach of his hands. And he is almost foolishly "local," heavy with particulars, to the point of seeming a busybody, a gossip, a flatterer, he is after things so. They laugh at him, that he is so little interested in their pother over power, however much he is interested in them—they feel that, and that he is more interested in them as men, as persons, than anyone else is.

It can be put this way, the dance, to key it: it is a wide investigation into the local, the occasional, what you might even call the ceremonial, but without, on Apollonius' part, any assurance that he knows how to make objects firm, or how firm he is. He is troubled, to cause objects to stay in place, to see clearly his place (the complicating factor of the opposite will at work around him is devilish to keep clear of, to stay clear about). The problem is, how to extricate what he wants from the mess he is surrounded by, how to manage to locate what he himself feels: that life as spirit is in the thing, in the instant, in this man. And then to fix it, in such a way that no one can see him act or hear him talk without, from that illumination, knowing how rich their own life is, and without

necessary reference to, any distracting contraries (which in any
case—he is sure of that—go on and on). In his trouble, in his
anger, and in his certainty, *Apollonius cries out:*

> The whole earth is mine, to journey through it—
> as is my life. Look, how handsome it is, how lovely
> the tongue is, behind the jumping teeth!
> > Otherwise,
> what is left you, but to shut yourselves up at home
> like fattening birds, and gorge your bellies in the dark,
> until you burst, with fat?

A DANCE OF PASSAGE, before MOVE four

He backs up on himself: from Cadiz he comes back through
the long Mediterranean to Tyana. He is doing what Odysseus
did before him, when he came away from Calypso's Island. But
in the interim of those 1000 years, the Mediterranean has grown
more self-conscious and so, more confusing—more people, but
less wise a place, perhaps. In any event, Apollonius moves back-
ward on a deeper plane of conjecture than the curiosity which
marked his coming into the Mediterranean. It is not so much
that he has lost any of the curiosity (the more intense a man is,
the more curious he is, but the more curious, the more the
curiosity is inside, is less obvious, looks masked, even sometimes
looks like diffidence). In Apollonius' case, the difficulty of
figuring out how to get across what is now the full content of
his person is so presented to him—he is so confronted—that he
moves differently. The lighting (the colors) can help here if they
are changed by graying from the primary, or "map" tones. Or
by some massing of them. For the real bother—the new thing
Apollonius knows—is quantity: he now understands (what it
has been so long necessary to understand) that the quantitative
increase of the number of men, of the number of goods, of the
known earth is not merely more of same but amounts to—when

it gets too large—a qualitative change, unless the vision of man, by admitting this shift of base quantity involves, restates itself to offset the loss. What Apollonius saw, by covering the known world—by hanging from the First Bridge at Byzantium (what was to be Constantinople), by watching the sea traffic at Alexandria (as you now watch it at Manhattan), by prowling the streets of Rome—was that two ills were coming on man: (1) unity was crowding out diversity (man was getting too multiplied to stay clear by way of the old vision of himself, the humanist one, was getting too distracted to abide in his own knowing with any of his old confidence); and (2) unity as a goal (making Rome an empire, say) had, as its intellectual pole an equally mischievous concept, that of the universal—of the "universals" as Socrates and Christ equally had laid them down. Form (which, from the first cities, had stuck by the glue of content to particulars) was suddenly swollen, was being taken as a thing larger a thing outside a thing above any particular, even any given man. And the whole business squatted on Apollonius as a wrong, somehow. He felt in himself that the very notion of goal was false, that to assume that there was any way that end could be separated from instant (from any person or object as any more than the exact striking of that person or object directly and presently on you or me) was as threatening an attack on the roots of life (as a man is life) as was the sucking up into itself by Rome of the function of distribution. Yet he had no answer—yet. He merely had the stubborn sense, with no false arrogation, that he and Tyana were bound together and that that binding was an image of health in the world. He had earlier found that his body and his mind could not be conceived as separable from each other. Now he took it that man and his world too were a sheaf at the harvest, just as seed and the earth were blackly joined in the growing.

So his return to Tyana, this time, is the major one. He has been out, and he comes back with none of the swift illumina-

tion (it was an easier part) he had brought back from Bagdad
and from Antioch. He is now 40 years old, and at last aware of
the dimension of his job: how to offer man a correction which
will restore (1) point by point sharpness; and (2) what he knows
makes such sharpness—the allaying of any doubt in a man that
he belongs, the restoration to him of the sense that everything
belongs to him to the degree that he makes himself responsible
for it as well as for himself. And Tyana, as his given, as a first
fact (no more than that, but no less) looms for him, at this junc-
ture, as in some way intimately connected with the job.

So there is a dance of passage here, a touching before
Apollonius once more goes on—for the last time. As he comes
back now (as he is pulled back) Tyana expresses the urgency
(recognizes it) by rising for the first time, and in the very
slowest large movements (no more than great turnings in place)
greets him. The actor of Tyana should turn as a stem or trunk
might be imagined to turn from the coursings of itself, not at all
human but most animate. The danger is, to keep all human, or
bough reference out of the arms (any feeling of embrace).
Tyana here, in contrast to their movement together on the floor
at the beginning of the play, should not touch or look at Apollonius, or let her arms have any overt part in her relevance to
him. What we should see, suddenly, is Tyana's change—that
Tyana has been changed by Apollonius' actions away from her:
it is he, his demand on himself and on life, that has made his
birthplace capable of verticality (his wish was, always, to be
known as "The Tyanean" and to be called "Apollonius of
Tyana"). Verticality, anyway, is the proper way a human body
can indicate penetration downward (not by lying down, or
crawling around on the ground, as so many do, who do not
understand): dignity, after all, is as much a sinking of the feet
into the earth as it is containment of the round of the self. And
Tyana's turning should have this quality of legs in the earth, and
none of the nonsense of clay, or return to dust, or of roots as

black and wet and gross. Just black. (It is necessary to empha-
size these things because dance, except as one or two are prac-
tising it—who understand that it is not mimesis but kinesis
which is its base—is altogether too descriptive and so is—of all
things for dance to be!—nonactive.)

Apollonius, for his part, also dances without eyes for Tyana.
He dances around her, the two being joined together rather by
the tensions established between them structurally than by any
references (psychological or literary) to each other. They both
are properly blind, non-descriptive and at the same time non-
mystical: there is no search in this thing (it is better if the
actors think of themselves as electronic, as magnet and field,
solely, so that they may act out the working out of the function, conjecture). For they both have the same thing on their
minds: how Apollonius can get down, get rid of all upstairs,
even the finest, even the flights of his mind, even the lyricism
(the Beautiful Thing) of his body.

Let Tyana be stem, huge turning solid, and let him be finding
out how to be likewise, but as a human being is stem (as place
never is). His arms assert multiple planes, the multiple horizon-
tals the vertical makes possible, and his legs the multiple vertical struts, so that, together, these two, make a dance of the
sphere of subject and object which Apollonius now has the
vision of—as the only full vision capable of delivering man
from his split.

As the dance ends, Tyana should go down, and Apollonius
himself replace her as the center—for she has enabled him to
understand, that what he has not done, with all his concentration, is to commit himself.

MOVE four

In this new confidence, Apollonius goes off from Tyana along
upper stage left, that is, East, straight East. He should move in
larger strides than he has yet used, and the colors of Persia,

Afghanistan, and India should come on much more rapidly than
did the colors of the other countries, more rapidly and more
thickly, perhaps, if that is possible.

                     INDIA, which he moves to,
should be almost an immediately recognizable place to him, in
that quick way any of us seize the thing which is right for us,
the thing which has been sitting inside us and waiting, suddenly, for its objectification. What Apollonius found there was
what he knew: that here was a will which asserted itself in-
ward, a sort of will the West had lost the law of, and so, only
turned it outward.

And when Apollonius was asked, later, in Egypt, by the
priests—the same priests from whom Herodotus took up, from
whom Plato got his myths, and Pythagoras admitted he learned
the secret of secrecy—when they asked Apollonius "Who is wise
enough to reform the religion of the Egyptians," he answered,
"Any sage who comes from India."

                               And what he
said he saw in India was what he learned there:

                     "men dwelling
on the earth, and yet not slaves of it, but lovers; I saw
them defended on all sides and yet without any defence,
I saw men possessed of nothing but what all possess."

And so the dance of India is *a dance of recognition.* St.
Augustine said of his experience of recognition, "It was a con-
flagration of myself," but with Apollonius the terms stay physical in another way, and in that way are neither light nor fire—
with him it is a burning, surely, but with nothing consumed,
on the contrary, it is as the action of the sun on us and on
things, increase is the issue, more growth, more life, more life,
leaves, men.

It is from his visit to India that Apollonius' only known
personal rite dates: his habit was to separate himself from
others three times in a day, at dawn, at noon, and at sundown,

to pay his respects, those times, to the sun, to source.

I see no reason why, just here, the dancer should not show, in his movements, exactly that sort of increase of his powers which Classic Indian dance offers any Western dancer—that in no better way can he indicate the sudden power Apollonius takes up than to use such things as (1) a new ability to move by the pulling of the toes alone; (2) by the directioning of the eyes (those night-trained eyes of an Indian dancer which, like a juggler's hands, can keep attention where he pleases); (3) the turkey-neck freeing of the head from the shoulders; and (4) that sinuosity an Indian dancer gets into his arms, so that they move from the bottom of the spine, and are as wings are simultaneously as they are as snakes.

II

The Apollonius who leaves India does not return to Tyana. He does not need to. He is now as fully empowered as man can be, and to the degree that he is so, the dance play shifts: all is now not the action of his shaping himself but he shaping others. He brings his vision to bear in two ways: (1) he wars against Caesarism (and the "universals" which lead to it and which it promotes) by working every way to affect and change emperors and kings, all ruling forces; and (2) he strikes at unity (and the immortalism he takes it such doctrine leads to) by teaching men everywhere, that what is native to themselves, even the places, heroes, and gods local to their neighborhoods, is worth all the state or world religions they are being offered on every hand. And the clue to both attacks is his prime conviction, that *no man should impose his mode of life on others.* (In advising the Indian rajah Phraotes to avoid proselytizing, Apollonius' argument was, it would estrange the rajah too much from his subjects, and when Vespasian asked him how to be a good emperor, Apollonius answered, "In what concerns yourself, act as a private man; in what concerns the state, act likewise." And

so he warned Vespasian to beware of taxes and of executions—
"Do not lop off," he said, "the ears of corn which show beyond
the rest.")

The dance problem is now great. This very code of Apollonius is contrary to drama as we have known it, in which the
events are will, are interference with others, are imposings,
either of the hero or on the hero or heroine. Here, in these final
actions of Apollonius, the reverse is true, it is another sort of
will and another sort of action, is drama as Noh is, as the Odyssey was and all the like single actor drama before it reaching
back to the Sumerian *epos*. So there is a new sort of learning
involved here, and I shall try to aid the dancer by increasing the
concreteness of the "situations," by documenting the two ways
Apollonius acts, and leave to the dancer what, of the story, he
shall use.

A DANCE OF PASSAGE, before MOVE five

                                        The first dance after India,
however, offers both a climax to what has preceded it as well as
an entrance to what follows. For in Egypt, where Apollonius
goes directly, on the Upper Nile he finds a community of men
who call themselves the GUMNOI, or, THE NAKEDS. It is just
such a "fix" as he is after—in the West, in the very area he wants
to fight generalization, a huge city of people (like a pueblo in its
rudeness—or like Yenan was) who are living together (men,
women and children: none of that celibacy) for purposes of
commitment, to allow themselves time and place for what they
take it life is, preoccupation with itself. (It is this end which has
led them, independent of him, to call themselves, the NAKEDS.)
At the same time, there is no arbitrary separation from life's
details, its daily mechanisms, nor is there any arrogation of race
or any excluding: Apollonius finds that the people themselves
are a mix of generations of Egyptians, Arabs and Ethiopians,
and that they live together without public conflict. They main-

tain the private principle by assigning, to each family, its own *hiera,* or cell.

All Apollonius does, all the dancer needs to do, is to dance a sort of happiness, a "Naked" happiness, non-interference with others, not so much ecstatic as we know ecstatic, but what ecstatic is, the discipline and joy of anyone when he or she has come to see that compulsion is no good, that nothing is so good as each allowed to be himself alone in the midst of the phenomenal world raging and yet apart. Apollonius dances in such joy, for these NAKEDS have taken up direct from energy where he believes it is, a part of the *daimonos* (which is also become a false word, but it is what Apollonius told his friend, the Roman consul Tellesinus, he knew wisdom to be, "The recognition of the daemonial nature in anything, including ourselves, and only these guileless paths give health").

All that Apollonius does, beyond enjoying these people (he stayed ten years with them, and one of his chief followers, Nilus, came from them), is to do, for the first time here, what he does from then on throughout the ancient world. Let me put it there.

MOVE five is two dances, the two acts, Part I THE RESTORA-TION OF THE LOCAL and Part II THE REMINDER TO THE EMPEROR HE IS PRIVATE MAN

Part I is a continuation directly out of the end of the NAKEDS' dance, and the dancer should make a progression out of it from Egypt by way of Paphos, Pergamus, Troy and Eleusis (the documentation is below) to Rome (where Part II takes place, also documented below). I suggest this because, whatever the differences of Apollonius' local actions, the dance itself is essentially one dance: in each instance Apollonius' assumption is that any image around which any people concentrate and commit themselves is a usable one just because it is theirs, that truth is never more than its own action, and that all that ever needs attention is the quality of the action.

Apollonius should dance throughout *to* the audience (as he has not had reason to, before, all previous movement, to whatever degree, being dis-covery of or the involvement of, himself). But now he can, and at Paphos the audience is the priests, at Pergamus his own old teachers, at Troy Achilles, and at Eleusis the Athenians, wor-shippers of Demeter and Persephone.

Documentation for Part I

(1) *Paphos:* the worship of Aphrodite—she is represented by a stone symbol the size of a human being and shaped like a pine cone, only smooth; the chief ritual is the tending of a flame of fire *(ancient phallic worship intact)*

(2) *Pergamus:* the new center of Aesculapian-Pythagorean doctrines—"healing," and chiefly by the prescriptive use of dreams *(ancient physio-psychic curing intact)*

(3) *Troy:* the tomb of Achilles. The story goes, Apollonius spent a night there, and in a dream was told by Achilles that the cult of Palamedes (who is said to have been the Greek who completed the alphabet as Kadmos the Phoe-nician brought it to Greece, and thus a culture hero of first importance) needed repair. Achilles told Apollonius where to find the grave in Thessaly, and Apollonius did find it, and did arouse the Thessalians to restore the old accustomed rites to the hero

(ancient culture hero rites restored)

(4) *Eleusis:* the temple to Demeter & Persephone—Apollon-ius was admitted to the rites, and is said, from his special knowledge of chthonic rites elsewhere (Delphi, Dodona, the cave of Trophonius, and in Asia generally) to have increased the priests' understanding of the animal fetish-ism of the worship (both the pig & the snake) and the sig-nificance of the underground "marriage"

(ancient chthonic, & mother-daughter rites)

Note: The mark of all of Apollonius' actions in Ionia and Greece is his care to slight the Olympian gods in favor of the older and more local heroes and divinities. At the same time there are notable rejections by him of all grossness: he refused to visit the labyrinth of the Bull-God of Crete, at Athens he spoke against effeminacy of the Bacchanalia and against the barbarities of gladiatorial combats, and writing to the priests at Delphi against blood-sacrifice, he said, "Heraclitus was a sage, but even he, and 660 years ago at that, never advised the people of Ephesus (whom he took for mud even though they were his kinsmen) to wash out mud with mud!"

MOVE five, Part II, THE DANCE OF, AND AGAINST, RULERS

It is one of the remarkable things about Apollonius, how kings, and the Roman emperors, were beholden to him, how much, actually, in the last third of his life, he was Confucian about such things as his responsibility for the body politic. His influence was enormous, and Vespasian, writing his last letter to his son Titus, reminds him, "We two emperors are solely what we are owing to the good advice of Apollonius." Nerva, too, used him, but Nero and Domitian were his enemies and in both these cases Apollonius had to risk his neck to keep at his work among people. Nero forbade him Rome in AD 66 (it was then that Apollonius went to Cadiz) but before he left, when he was being questioned by Nero's agents, he warded off one dangerous thrust. One of the questioners tried to trap him by asking, "What do you think of Nero?" And he answered: "I think better of him than you do, for you think he ought to sing, and I think he ought to keep silent."

When Domitian actually put him on trial, all Apollonius' friends urged him to flee, that his chance to escape death was small. His answer was, that there is always "the moment that suits wisdom best to give death battle," and this seemed to be it, and he gave it. He was acquitted, and there is no better way to give the dancer a sense of the dimension of his subject, in such a situation, than to give Apollonius' reasonings on why he stood up to Domitian:

> The law obliges us to die for liberty, and nature ordains that we should die for our parents, our friends, or our children. All men are bound by these duties.
>
> But a higher duty is laid upon the sage. He must die for his principles and the truth he holds dearer than life. It is not law that lays this choice upon him, it is not nature. It is the strength and courage of his own soul. Though all threaten him, he will not give away nor shall force force from him the slightest falsehood. He will guard the secrets of others' lives and all that has been trusted to his honor as religiously as the secrets of initiation. And I know more than other men, for I know that of all that I know, I know some things for the good, some for the wise, some for myself, some for the Gods, but none for tyrants.
>
> Again, I think that a wise man does nothing alone or by himself: no thought of his is so secret, for he has himself as witness to it. And whether the famous saying "know thyself" be from Apollo or from some sage who learnt to know himself and proclaimed it as a good for all, I think the wise man who knows himself and has his own spirit in constant comradeship, to fight at his right hand, will neither cringe at what the vulgar fear nor dare to do what most men do without the slightest shame.

So long as Domitian ruled (AD 81-96) Apollonius kept up his attacks on him. He was visiting Ionia when Domitian was murdered, was at Ephesus, actually, and was speaking at a small park in a suburb of that city at the time murder was taking place in Rome (as was found out afterwards). It was midday, and just then Apollonius broke off, troubled, took three or four steps forward, and definitely out of context cried out, "Strike the tyrant, strike."

THE DISAPPEARANCE, or end of the play

It is here, just here at Ephesus, death of Domitian, date AD 96, that Apollonius disappears. And it has usually been left as a sort of proper ending to a holy man's life. But I want this dance to read back into the record just what happened. He had done his work. He was near home. And with pride and ease, let the dancer go back to Tyana, let him come in slow to her as she sits as she sat at the beginning of the play, and let him come down to her, go forward into her arms, and as the lights go down, the color over the whole stage area (the known world) should first go off, color by color, and then, when the same stick of light with which the play opens is all that picks out the two of them, let that light go down, showing us the two of them as they were, but with this one difference, that, now Apollonius's back is to the audience, and they shape together an ambiguous, double-backed thing as darkness returns and is final.

DOCUMENT

a play written for the dining hall of
Black Mountain College, January 23, 1952

The chief elements of the area to be here used are:
THE FIREPLACE
& THE FIRST FOUR POSTS
The dominant lighting is to be a live fire burning throughout the
play, that fire to be kept throughout by anonymous figures
squatting around it like any campfire—with this exception, that,
they speak together certain choral responses.

The chief actors are to be eight, two sibs to each of the four
posts, a speaker and a dancer for each. The speaker of each is to
be bound to it, & to stay until that time when the thongs of
some of them are to be burned off (from a flame from the fire)
by the dancer of that post.

There shall, however, be another lighting local to the distinguish-
ing environment of each of the posts (the intent is, to maintain
the back area—that is, the fireplace & its keepers—as the presid-
ing archaic force—it is the center slot for the audience—; at the
same time that the forward plane made by the four posts is the
"present," or, "daily" reality). So each of the four posts should
have a lighting (if manageable, not so much a spot but an area
hewn out by color slides—by projections) proper to the
problems of the individuals of each post.

The source of this lighting is not to be left as the dead mechanics
of a projection booth but is to be the third of the planes of the
production. There are to be two actor-lighters either in bosun's
chairs hung from the light-bar or in crow's nests constructed at
the top of posts 5 & 6. They shall be interrogators or challeng-
ers of the speakers of the four posts, not choral but direct, indi-
vidualized speakers to speakers.

The picture, then, is this:

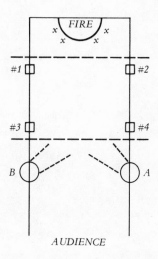

The play opens with all actors in position before the audience comes into the hall, so that they enter into a dark hall to take their seats (the assumption is that the light from the fireplace will be enough to show them the way to their chairs, but if this isn't enough there shall be ushers standing at the door with flashlights so beamed as to direct the audience to go to the seats).

The figures at the four posts shall be moving—the only figures moving—and moving (as far as their entanglements allow) in equivalences to the flames lighting them from the fire. ((It is apparent that just here the music of the production is the quieter of the audience and the starter of the play's mood. I would favor reeds, would like one or two shakuhachi, say, to do the first soundings—with single voices cutting in to the instruments from the figures around the fire, not words but hummings, statements, phrases pitched to the shakuhachi:

(phase 1)

   X^1: "not night"
           X^2: "not now"
                    X^3: "or night"
                             X^4: "or now"

(phase 2)

   X^1: "light"
           X^2: "any time"
                    X^3: "makes more dark"
                             X^4: "is, the problem"

(phase 3)

   X^1: "the fire is"
           X^2: "the time is"
                    X^3: "what is obscure is"
                             X^4: "*now* is"

(phase 4, &
making a sentence)

   X^1: "I am
           X^2: . . . forever is
                    X^3: light is:
                             X^4: NOW!"

((*Note to the composer & the director:* there should be
no hurry to anything. Each phrase should be most distinct, & each phase left to hang in its own air.

                                     The point
of this opening is: voices. The part of the drone, as well
as the constant of the drum, I have imagined as not
starting until the creatures of the posts begin the more

active part of the play.

> The "style" sought, in both the music & the voices, is what an Indian would call Dhrupada: the static or heroic beauty of music & of man.

> The sentiment (the right raga of the shakuhachi should make it possible) is the joint one, love-and-valor.

> The text itself declares both the time and the season.

> A repetition of the whole passage would seem to me no loss at all, giving the audience its chance to be accustomed to the darkness, & what light.))

The drone instrument's coming in shifts the attention from the opening and is the preparation for the emergence of Post figure & dancer #1. (The dancer, during the first words, is hidden from the audience on the up-stage side of the post.)

#1 is—to the extent that these notes may be more symbolic than any performance should be—a man as a part of any of our natures is a tree. I would, therefore, be careful that this role is played by a male, precisely because such movement is usually conceived of as feminine. (#2, which is notated as that of us all which is rock-like, resistant, should, vice-versa, be spoken and danced by women, these chiasmic methods are essential to the proper effects of the play and of its production.)

So, emerging from the opening, #1 is bound up, say, to the knees—perhaps to the ankles only. And *sway* is the characteristic motion of both the speaker and the dancer, the ultimate skill of it being that, at the heights of its effort to express & be free of its statements, it sways so singularly from the bound ankles that it is as a tree against its roots in storm. This is the climax. The beginning is arms, shoulders, chest, fingers, hands,

leaves & boughs. Trunk is medial. The end is the effort to leave
the root.

　　　(This being so bound seems to me of such essence that,
in this case—Post #1—I think the dancer of the double role
should not ever go away from the post, should, in fact, be only
the more treeness of the human individual that the speaker is.)

#1 speaks:
　　　I would be light
　　　as milkweed settling,
　　　I would be sweet
　　　as hay is: I would be
　　　free

　　　　　　　　　　　Lightman A:

　　　　　　　　　　　　　　Ha! free! he sez,
　　　　　　　　　　　　　　free! Who'z
　　　　　　　　　　　　　　what that is, now—
　　　　　　　　　　　　　　or ever waz?

　　　　　　　　　　　(This coming in should be sud-
　　　　　　　　　　　den, a rasp, as he brings on to the
　　　　　　　　　　　figure of #1 as lovely a yellow
　　　　　　　　　　　light as a slide—no commercial
　　　　　　　　　　　amber, a new made slide—can
　　　　　　　　　　　produce.
　　　　　　　　　　　　　　The voice should be a
　　　　　　　　　　　lovely ugly one—the present, the
　　　　　　　　　　　flat, sharp anti-poetic present.)

#1:
　　　I would be open, able
　　　to take each changing
　　　as even a weed stands
　　　the rain's
　　　thrashing, as well as the sun's
　　　quietness, or the cloud's
　　　chill

Lightman A:

    ya. will:
    he wants to be
    without will

    hey, Will-ie (tossing it
      across to Lightman B)

    this guy wants
    to be what nobody
    ain't

#1:

    plumey, perky
    dark & tangled,
    flamey—clumps
    of Christmas
    rose

    A:
    Willie, what's
    to be a
    rose?

    What's this guy's
    problem?

There is no answer from Lightman B. Instead, he brings up a
white light on Post #2, disclosing figure #2. It is made up of
both the speaker and the dancer [. . .]

TELEPINUS

a Christmas Entertainment for Manhattanville

The Presenter   Solstice: at such time
I was born and die
each equinox.
We are to be merry now.
The leisure class
has been done away
The masses
are all over the place
The socialists
are banging at the door
We are to be merry now

        The moon is new
        the tide is rising
        the ship is winding,

we are to be merry now
we are to go
we are to have something
to do

wintertime
has sat down
the sun
has gone away
I was born
when the sun was away
I was three
when the sun was away
with spring and fall
I die

I hate the decisions
of the middle class
the hope
of the futile masses
I don't believe the socialists
will ever catch up with agriculture
I am merry now. Are you?

Enter Joseph   The sun comes back
& brings spring
bursts the berry
I am Joseph

I am Joseph
none of these worries
trouble me
Equinox, my hat

I am an everlasting
class. I do
and do. I simply
go on I am

Joseph
I am
the berry
bully
for me—
I'm not
happy.
I am

The sun
only goes
so far
I am Joseph
Who are you?

The Chorus   booie for you
a group on
stage like
the audience

The Presenter   This is not funny
                      I am not merry
                      Too many people
                      all over the place

                      No hope when more
                      are made every day
                      something new
                      in every store

                      itchy people
                      with more & more
                      & socialists
                      banging with wristwatches
                      on every door

                      are you merry
                      at Christmas tide?
                      I've gone south
                      on the sun's
                      ride

The Chorus   booie for you

Enter Anthony   I am Anthony
carrying a   Francis
child   Harry
                      I'm every child's
                          uncle

No child
  is a
peduncle
  so
every child

has to have
  one like me or

every mother
has to have
a sonny boy
  like me to

carry
  Charlie
  Tommy
  Joe
—I am Anthony

from head
  to toe
good as no

one ever was
  to hold the
child up
  by his us

there goes I
  good old
saint
  Anthon-ý

Chorus   aaaa
                      this gets too
                      ha-ha: who
                      cares for the figure

                      now, who's merry
                      at all at the
                      thought of
                      season

                      who gives a damn
                      that anyone's born?
                      who worries
                      that anything dies?

                      We'll make it new
                      for you tomorrow
                      you can buy it right now
                      & go back in your house

                      the sun's only there
                      for a kick for the universe
                      & man's only born
                      for a ball

                      are you on, man
                      or out to lunch?
                      we are to go
                      what's next?

Enter Mary   I am the cherry
                        rosy & red
                        I am the Mary
                        of the son who bled

                        You are all relaxed
                        in your midget cars
                        or messed up good
                        in communes

Don't look now
but I'm having another

and it ain't
under cover

it ain't exponential,
either

> I am the cherry
> rosy & red
> if you can read me
> I'm dead

Chorus [blank / stuck—leaves thing as is]

Enter Doctor, cool
having been painting
the walls of his house
green

studies heartline on film presented by
nurse   makes notes   indicates

to Telepinus [who had been Presenter] hold up
   arm
takes blood pressure   examines

ears   puts light in eyes   opens

mouth   prescribes

[prescription   scloromiazine   says nothing
can be shown   throughout   leaves patient
on large card
held up by   satisfied   dressing
nurse]   quietly as Doctor
goes back to painting
walls bedroom-green

Enter Ass
on which Joseph took Mary
to Egypt, alone
classical two-man horse
only looking like sd Ass

        I am the Ass
     who went to Egypt
     where would I go
     today?

        Look whom I've got
     on my back
          [bumpy business of Anthony
            trying to mount him]

    another ass
    uncle himself

        I'm doing a dance
    because we're supposed
    to be going
         ahead

            [at which point dance
              like rodeo in which
              Anthony is dumped
              & is dragged off
              as horse exits
              by man of rear
              end sticking out
              hand & hauling
              him off—the Good One—
              by his tonsor
              what hair he can get a
              hold of]

Telepinus enters
  immediately
  carrying
Mary & Joseph
before & behind
like a Japanese
  wrestler

[acting here, all:
reverse of previous
scene—big firm
action; one turn
at center stage
to face Chorus so
audience sees
tripartite figure
on angle and his
back, possibly
additional turn
toward audience so
face seen also like
two-men-on-a-horse:
figure only the point]

Exit, with Chorus
closing

The sun has turned
this winterday
Telepinus
has unwound

What happens
next you best
can tell
when you come back

again,
what do you think
how merry now
you might perchance
might be

the year is new
the century old
that was Telepinus
went

come back
another year
yourselves
and see

END ENTERTAINMENT

FLUFF

a "Temperament" of Four Natures

for Leon Katz, of Manhattanville
to do with as he wants

NATURE BOY (little unattractive-attractive male—
that kind of cocky):
    I am nature
    with my club
    I'm all the wildness
    everyone wants
    a ball let's go
    I rend & push
    I toss make sloppy
    have a ball I   [actions
    am break-out   accordingly: all
    & rubbish   rumpus as befits
    I can hook   as well the others
    anybody   below:
    Don't you want   'dance'
    to go I mean   positions
    travel   posturing
    make a journey   faces
    go?   fingers leaps
        bent over
    all uglinesses.

LADY 1:
    I am nature
    with my softness
    I am the kitten
    to her bitch [indicating Lady #2 to come, or also
        all four on stage waiting to step
        forth to get theirs?]

I can mix
fingers
with
anything
I can wiggle
under any
hairy
matter
I can touch
anybody
loose   [collapsing
I am   into
wiggle   its own
 ass   rottenness
Doris
Day
I am pastry
in your stomach
I am
bullshit
all over

HYACINTHUS (blond attractive male):
I am nature
what about personal touch?
I know how
to make anyone
feel good
All I have to do
is lean over them
& talk to them
as though they also
are real like
me. I don't think

anyone isn't
valuable. I use
democracy
If I'm not
playing tennis
I'm talking
to someone
I can make
anything
perk up
I'm
an entertainer
par excellence
I can drive
men & women
crazy by
coming close
to them
I don't believe
in anything
I don't believe
in you

[by which point the grossness of all
four of these ought to be now so
apparent they can begin to mix
business, all piling on & off each
other like dogs in a gangbang, the
final girl's speech—and the end of
it—ought to make for a brawl

LADY 2:

I am nature
what about me—I mean
me   Look at
me admirare
If you give me attention
I know you like me

Don't look now
but I'm looking for that
If I don't get attention
I am depressed
If you'll like me
I'll love you
if you don't
    beat me
I'm ipsus
    mysus
up side down
turn me over
& spank me

END–IN BRAWL
with LADY 2 getting it from all 3,
literally, a vulgar dirty mess

WHITE ISLE, IN THE BLACK SEA

a short play for Manhattanville

Chorus
Mimus
Achilles
Helen
Neoptolemus
sailors
& music

Chorus (in full spotlight at rear of stage and full face to audience

> 'stating' but almost like
> shrieking (though *not* at all)

> [cf. music—*per Boulez*—
> possible here as
> *necessary below*]

hang the most beautiful woman in the world
from a tree
dip the handsomest warrior likewise
in the boiling bronze
put them together on an island in the sea
& they shall make songs come out to sailors' ears
will stop their ships as they stand
and the clash of weapons on weapon
shall be as the washing of clothes

no man shall stay after sunset
no woman shall stray on to the island at all

but if there are those who have wounds
& don't know the string pulls out of the ulcer
they shall go to the island in the daytime
and one or the other of the persons there,
Helen or Patroclus or Achilles
will tell you if you are dumb
how to speak

then cut, & there is Achilles & Helen as light as lovers sitting
dandling as if by a pool (only it is the whole Black Sea in front
of them) *singing separately:*

   A: as the bronze fell on my side

   H: as I loved the adulterer as well

   A: as I fell by Apollo's secret blow

   H: as I fled from Orestes still seeking to wipe out
        his father's blood guilt

   A: as my body wasn't there
        when I fell

   H: as I believed my friend Polyxo

   A: as I was picked up by which goddess

Achilles continuing (to side)

      did my mother
      recur to cover
      what she had
      neglected

                              Helen, to side or as much
                              direct to audience, either one
                              of them changing from the
                              antiphone:

> I know now Polyxo
> thought I had touched
> her husband because
> each man desired me

Helen and Achilles continuing together:

> these wildnesses are now
> not so interesting that excesses
> occur in all instances

H: not the specialty of my beauty

A: not the specialty of my beauty

H: not the specialty of my power

A: not the specialty of my power

Helen and Achilles continuing together:

A: not one single person any more
  ghosts in the line where the fighting is
H: self-consciousness in the woman's beauty
  where the beauty is

Chorus interrupting rudely:

> hang the most beautiful woman in the world

> dip the handsomest warrior likewise

Mimus, coming from
a back of the stage
distinct from the Chorus
like a single chorus
(to which he retires when
finished):

It happened to these two people that they did get
here after all. One was Achilles and he did not die he
disappeared at the moment he fell. He'll have more to
say later about what happened to him. And Helen—
everybody thinks they know what happened to her.
Except this—that here she is—as Achilles' wife—on
this island in the Black Sea. It came about this way:
Menelaus was dead and she was forced to flee because
Orestes was still trying to complete that wild blood-
feud of his over his father's death and by the quirk
that by this time he has Helen blamed for starting the
war at all. She had to go, and went to Rhodes where
she thought that the girl who grew up with her,
Polyxo, would save her, but the moment the chance
came Polyxo had her maidens seize Helen and hang
her from a tree. It was thus she died—or rather they
hung her, and she came to this isle.

Sailors interrupt putting ashore Neoptolemus—preferably, they
and he come directly out of the audience—the man who smells
the worst in the world from the bite of a serpent in his heel
which is wrapped in an ordinary dirty bandage as he becomes
the 3rd principal on the stage

Achilles to him (in horror at the odor):

> why do you come here
> who have been the curse
> of each place you've been?

> why do you come now
> after all is over
> —all that had shape, & meaning?

Neoptolemus:

> I come because I am excessive
> I am the ghost of Neoptolemus
> spread now in each place
>
> I was told to come to you
> to you both in all the world
> as the only place where healing
>
> has some meaning some end
> to the shapelessness of my leg
> to the hidden terror of my own
>
> sore. I come to you to be
> healed by song I came
> to listen to you both

(*Helen moves in,* showing no horror at the odor from Neoptolemus, and her step forward is no more than the grace of the greatest hostess of the ancient world.)

Achilles, to Neoptolemus:

> can a man heal another but I can say
> where I went: the earth swallowed me
> I passed close to Persephone on the edge
> of hell

Helen:

> and as he skirted her I, independently,
> was Persephone myself: when I hung
> from the tree and watched him
> in his agony

Achilles:

> I sank in the ground literally
> of my place   I gave up all
> that was golden of me
> It was Apollo
> who had guided Alexander's arm
> to take my life from me

Helen:

> a woman of beauty
> has that excess of power
> I had had no reason
> to turn my power in.
> No man on earth
> would have refused me
> all women enjoyed my
> beauty

Achilles:

> I was immediate
> she was all
> Neoptolemus,
> all flaw,
> what are you?

Mimus steps forward and says:

> Neoptolemus was the son of Hercules but Hercules
> had so many sons none of them knew him very much and
> Neoptolemus' mother had been left by Hercules. The one
> thing Neoptolemus did get from his father was the bow
> he's carrying, thereby causing him all his trouble because
> the Greeks it turned out were never going to beat Troy

without that bow. But meanwhile a snake had given him
this sore and he was forever being left alone by everybody.
The odor in the Greek camp in fact had got so bad he was
rowed out to a rock and left there for five years.

Mimus steps back, and the conversation continues

Neoptolemus:

> Leonymus told me he had struck
> at the empty place in the Locrian line
> where the ghost of Ajax was supposed to be
>
> mocking the belief anything has power
> except what is real. I'm
> the opposite: I've had this thing
>
> all my life, real as real,
> and I'd mock nothing but I wouldn't also
> know what snake it was, or why
>
> I have been this way. I come to you both
> to give me reason to think anything
> of myself except the real.
>
> Why are you, the most beautiful woman
>
> and you, the paragon of man,
> why are you wed
> on this White Island here
>
> in the midst of the sea?
> What is it that I am
> that is more than you?

Chorus:

> the grief of the man
> who has had no power
>
> the loneliness of a woman
> who does not have beauty
>
> the bow alone which everybody wants
> the sore which keeps everyone away
>
> Neoptolemus! *(as addressed to him as a cry*

Achilles, going right on:

> my mother
> held me up
> and the one place
> she held me by
> was untouched
> by the fire

Neoptolemus:

> I was weak
> in a like place
> but have no answer
> such as you

Achilles:

> It was where
> I was loose and eager

Neoptolemus:

> It was where
> I was dumb and blind

Chorus, breaking in with original angry voice:

    hang the suffering as well by their heels

    hang all deviation

    from health

Mimus steps forward:

    the bow was as the world

    in the clash of sword on sword

    in the parry of the shield

(sounds of same
as brilliant as song
off stage,
—literal music
composed for
same

(awakes Neoptolemus to his bow
which he has been carrying limply to now)

Mimus:

    look at him quicken

    from within

    at what shall he aim

    he's asking

        (even Achilles
        presents himself
        to Neoptolemus—in Neoptolemus' mind,
        & a-rousement—as a subject

        but of course the clash offstage
        is where the bow finally points)

(Achilles steps in front
of the brilliance of the
quick act of Neoptolemus
who is the son

Helen too quietly has
no trouble with
this sudden recurrence
of the danger of Orestes

and they both, by union,
as well as the same
dandling quality
of their original appearance

ease Neoptolemus.
Before their own eyes
and his own sense of himself
—that these two don't

block off, and have stepped
in front of the terrible bow—
he takes himself differently
on the moment

Helen (crying out):

    Neoptolemus, for the first time

    you are enchanted

Achilles:

    How different it was

    for me: it took me a long time

    to be disenchanted

Chorus (as the figures cease & set

       as the chorus does—&

       Mimus also

                  the same music obtains
                  for an instant in an opposite
                  of the same sounds—two,
                  & not clashing, sounding

                    as the Chorus

speaks a duplicate
of its opening:

    the sailors stop

    in the middle of the sea

    who pass by

    this island

    Neoptolemus is free   *(the sailors who landed him*
                           reappear, & show opposite
                           reactions as they take him off)

(Chorus continuing:)

a bird is seated with expanded wings

on the thigh of Achilles

Helen is cooled by the spray

END PLAY

WILD MAN FRAGMENT

start with a rumpus
start with a ball
what's in the railroad station
who's alone

Enter the WILD MAN shoulders & head covered with leaves, & a thorn-apple branch sticking out of his stomach; he is not shaggy but so far as it is humanly possible should be all lines as waves   his body like shock waves   vibrations moving[?] constantly both as outlines of him as veil (as much as it is possible) all his insides too

carrying club—a normal picked up reasonably thick branch—to keep off dogs & he has to, often, be parrying—keeping off— dogs; this is as much a part of his constant action as the previously described state of wave-like motion (ripples, like palsy almost)

a very attractive figure despite guise   very winning but a modality so little known   the problem of presenting him so that he isn't comic is going to be difficult (dance or immense control like a Yiddish Art Theatre actor, circum 1935, necessary: very suggestive role

He is nature, as truly as METROPOLIS (who shall soon occupy middle stage) also is, but as she is sedentary immense controlling in the opposite sense of static/inert   he is quick-vibration & brilliance of all mind which isn't intellectual [that part will soon enter right as POINTED BEARD, & be scientist   modernism commercial-success   present intellectual best (exponential IBM computer future), the full miserable self-autonomy of the intellectual as it now is].

WILD MAN: I am the man who slipped away
                 fell soft out of the game
                 right in the midst of the play
                 gave in to myself and looked
                 aside. I fell down into
                 the holes in the wood   I went off
                 where fear reigns   I was
                 the one that was missing
                 I was gone when there
                 Everything made me jump
                 I still walk the earth
                 happy but scared if
                 I meet anyone who is
                 a hostile spirit. And there
                 is much today which
                 is. It is very difficult
                 for me to go into
                 any place   Or take
                 the chance to see
                 someone I know. Rather
                 I'd see someone
                 new   go anyplace
                 other than I know
                          Etc

Enter right
POINTED BEARD: I am the king
                 of everything. I am the brightness
                 round[?] the earth.
                    I enjoy
                 music after hours
                 or on the job
                    I can do anything
                 in any circumstance

I am brightness
never was before,
never was free
to be as men
I am the maker
of all new goods
I guarantee
the future
I am the military
establishment
I am the commercial
success
I am the one
the race
will be
I am the newly
minted
I am
free

Sees WILD MAN and is full of disdain, treats him as a bother-
some dog. But WILD MAN is plenty protected by his own more
native (neolithic) powers which at least by stepping aside he has
been able to fall back on, foster like feelings—to begin to
foster—to be any longer ridden over readily by such press as
POINTED BEARD is so abnormally capable of expressing—execu-
tive shit but in such obvious abilities   the glare of his eye
alone, in its vanity, is a form of power; and that makes WILD
MAN shrink

Out of my way
dog of the past
We don't need any
of your slowness
a bit more,

            I'll take my
            auto-gyro
            & whir you
            over on the
            ground
            you leaf
            you dear dope

at which WILD MAN does lift his stick & POINTED BEARD folds
himself up just a trifle in his nervousness that he ain't got it all
made the way he thinks he has. But so far he is tops.

At which point center stage stirs out of a previous nonevident-
ness and the Figure of a most normal man is there . . . [breaks
off]

THE NINETEENTH OF APRIL

(The spirit here is Quimper plates, Giotto, and some prints contemporary to the action. The desire is to get a speed and delicacy of action as if Noh and movie were spliced together. No weight, and a shifting without hurry but which ought to give, at the end, a sense of continuousness despite all variety of a homogenous film—or 'flow' like a snowstorm. Action, and words, should be almost like dumb show or silence, rather than dramatic, leaving the exactness & literalness of all scenes—the realism —to make its own point without pointing. The 'pointing' in other words should be like words rather. For this is a verse-play! The attempt is to make history 'work'!)

SCENE 1 — the evening of the 18th of April, 1775, in the dining room of the Reverend Jonas Clarke, the old 'Hancock' mansion a half mile off the center of Lexington, in Massachusetts. Present, beside the host and his wife, are Aunt Hancock and Dorothy Quincy, and Dorothy Quincy's fiancé, Mr. John Hancock, with Samuel Adams the fifth person—or wheel, for Mr. Adams this night (in contrast to the next to the last scene— when he is in nadir) is now in the height and brilliance of his long previous unsuccessful meeting of the Massachusetts Provincial Congress and before the Second Continental Congress of Philadelphia, to which he and Hancock are expecting to leave within the next day or so. But as Adams sits this evening—the dinner is close to over—he is full of the power still to create events.

CLARKE is speaking: "It cannot be otherwise. Locke is right. Men are a set of beings naturally free. And they will fight when fighting has reason for its basis."

ADAMS: "I do believe. With a suitable quantity of flints . . .

two pieces of cannon . . . a pair of drums . . . bayonets. Where?
where shall it happen?"

    while HANCOCK is making a sly pass along below the edge of
the table at Miss Quincy, who rather pays attention to the other
two men, at the same time with her eye on the main target of
her present situation in life, this wealthiest man in the Colonies,
a saucy upstart rather more an 18th century rake—from his own
self-pleasure—than the Copley portrait. But then, he was as
much as he was and he ought to look with eyes rather too close
together and his set chin than as I say. For Sam Adams has
brought him a long way, and watches over him as a most valuable & usable property. But it is Hancock who will, within 24
hours, have started Adams down, & out. (Adams can look just
as he does, by Copley.)

    The scene declines in the shoving back of chairs.

SCENE 2 – Boston, the house of Dr. Joseph Warren, and he directing Paul Revere to leave to go to tell Hancock and Adams that the British are on the move.

REVERE speaks: "But Church *has* to be the spy."

WARREN: "True. But we will use him. The thing is, that to-night he can do us no harm. You are sure you can go through?"

Revere's assent is as much in the eye with which he regards Warren as any stiff nod of his head. The point of this scene anyway is to get these two men before the audience right at the start in anticipation—and in the full light of a house (doctor's) living room—of their appearance later. For they are a pair of a different doublet than Adams and Hancock. Both younger—and Copley's portrait of each is again the measure—Warren (34) a man it would be hard to tell the end of, if he wasn't to be killed at Bunker Hill; and Revere (40) the skilled workman above the mechanics, who will be revealed later in his own speech in the night in the pasture with the British officers off the road beyond Lexington on the way to Concord. Warren is rich in temperament, swift and kind, and so presents himself as, with Revere's nod—looking as he does, in Copley's portrait—hard eyed, a perpendicular nose right out of his forehead and a jaw to push a horse down, heels to go.

SCENE 3 — woods beyond Lexington off road to Concord. Revere, Dawes and Doctor Prescott (of Concord) having been stopped by British officers placed there by General Gage's plan, to intercept any word reaching Concord that the troops are coming. Prescott however, knowing the country, signals Revere to make a dash for it. Prescott gets away but Revere, going straight ahead into an orchard, plans to abandon his horse and hoof it across fields and country to Concord. In which he is surprised by another group of the British who are guarding previous men taken in just the orchard Revere has chosen, in the dark, to go into. In other words he walks right into their arms. The hour is about 1 AM.

The scene then opens with Revere on foot running in from stage left in as little light as necessary and is directly taken by a group of 3 or 5 British soldiers. The interrogation follows:

OFFICER: "Where do you come from?"

REVERE: "Boston."

OFFICER: "What time did you leave?"

REVERE: "About 11 o'clock."

OFFICER: "May I ask your name?"

REVERE: "My name is Revere."

OFFICER: "Paul Revere?"

REVERE: "Yes."

The other troops abuse Revere, calling him "Damn'd Rebel," jostling him, and sneering, "You're in for it, now."

But the OFFICER says: "Do not be frightened. We intend you no harm."

REVERE answers: "If they think they can they are mistaken."

OFFICER: "We are only posted to seize deserters."

REVERE: "That's a plausible story, I know better than that."

OFFICER: "No, there are British deserters reported on this road."

REVERE: "You are here to prevent surprise at Concord. I know what you are after. I have aroused the country all the way down, and they are now up in arms. And besides your own boats grounded crossing the Charles. That's what you don't know."

At which point the Officer changes his whole attitude and becomes completely alert to the advantage of the prisoner he has taken. But Revere pushes on with his information, to the point of course which he wants to reach, of the lie which he then tells, which, perhaps as much as anything—even more than Sam Adams' presence behind the scene of the battle—caused it.

REVERE: "I'll tell you another thing. I shall have 500 men at Lexington very soon."

With that the Officer runs off up the orchard and meanwhile the others jostle Revere until the Officer returns with a superior who enters to cock his pistol at Revere's head and say:

NEW OFFICER: "I'm going to ask you some questions and if you don't tell me the truth I'll blow your brains out."

REVERE: "I call myself a man of truth. You stopped me on the highway going about my business and made me a prisoner with no right or reason and now you question me with what right I know not. I will tell you the truth, for I am not afraid."

NEW OFFICER: "What time did you leave Boston?"

REVERE repeats: ["About 11 o'clock."]

NEW OFFICER: "And did you say the boats grounded?"

REVERE: "They did, before even they got out of Back Bay actually. And those which managed to get into the tide hung up on the Cambridge side."

(Pure bold lie, for Revere had left Boston hours before the British ever did parade, and were only out in the boats after he had left Charlestown himself, and was already in Lexington. But he knew from information received in Charlestown that such officers as he now was in the hands of had left Boston and moved casually down the road and through Lexington during the afternoon. So his guess and plant was shrewd and consequential.)

NEW OFFICER (after some glances and some mutterings with the other British): "And what is this of men at Lexington?"

REVERE: "It's true, I told all as I came by to gather there, all the militia of the several towns between Boston and here, Sir. And you shall find them there if you turn back. You are already trapped."

At which the Officer and the other and another speak together in low tones, Revere is searched but has no pistol and all go off from the woods toward the road.

OFFICER, to Revere: "We are now going toward your friends and if you attempt to run, or we are insulted, we will shoot you."

REVERE (sure that his work is done): "You may do as you please."

SCENE 4 — Lexington Green. ADAMS' voice: "Stand" The militia do, as a group—say 5, for the front line, if possible more, but on edge of stage left, suggesting other lines behind anyway, and with one officer, who looks, after Adams' voice has come as though from behind stage, and there is query and doubt on the officer's face as well as the men's. But at this point the British come on with guns lined to fire on stage right, with an officer who says, with command, to the militia: "Disperse." But just before the militia officer, as he has seen the ready guns of the British, has himself said, "We better go," and two or three of the five of the militia line have broken and turned away when the British volley occurs. Two of these fall shot in the back, and one of those left standing crumples and the leading British soldier bayonets him to finish the action. With one intervening moment before the British fire: in the light behind the action in center stage—a stonewall say may be suggested as there—a cocked pistol has flashed but only the flash, as much as though it was held straight up into the air: no discharge. But enough, with the eye of the British soldiers alert to everything in front and to the side of them, to be in fact the 'scare' to send off the volley. There is a scattered & unsuccessful fire back from the colonists—which can be the one remaining standing militiaman in front line with muskets from offstage firing also at the British. No effect.

SCENE 5 – burying ground Lexington, just after the 8 boxes (each made of 4 large boards nailed up) have been put down in one large trench placed near the woods (back of stage) as possible—clods now being thrown in as Reverend Clarke stands over the trench, with his wife alongside him carrying a 6 months old baby Sally in her arms, and with the 12 year old Elizabeth standing with them with eyes as big as etc—other townspeople suggested. It is a little rainy, and Clarke indicates pine and oak brush in the woods be brought to pile up over the trench so that the British will not find it because it looks like a heap of brush at that point of the burying-ground.

SCENE 6, and any more intended thereafter, unfinished.

FOUR SEASONS PAPERBACKS

Robert Creeley: *The Charm: Early & Uncollected Poems*
Contexts of Poetry: Interviews 1961-1971
A Quick Graph: Collected Notes & Essays

Edward Dorn: *The Collected Poems,* 1956-1974

Drummond Hadley: *The Webbing*

Dale Herd: *Early Morning Wind and Other Stories*

Philip Lamantia: *The Blood of the Air*
Touch of the Marvelous

Michael McClure: *Ghost Tantras*

Pamela Millward: *Mother, A Novel of the Revolution*

Charles Olson: *Additional Prose: A Bibliography on America,*
Proprioception & Other Notes & Essays
The Fiery Hunt, and other Plays
Muthologos: Collected Interviews and Lectures

David Schaff: *The Moon by Day*

Gary Snyder: *Riprap & Cold Mountain Poems*
Six Sections from Mountains and Rivers Without
End, Plus One

Charles Upton: *Time Raid*

Philip Whalen: *The Kindness of Strangers, Poems* 1969-1974
Severance Pay

Edward Conze (tr.): *The Perfection of Wisdom in Eight Thousand Lines*
& Its Verse Summary